P9-CEM-946

THRICE THROUGH THE VALLEY

VALETTA STEEL
with ED ERNY

LIVING BOOKS
Tyndale House Publishers, Inc.
Wheaton, Illinois

All Bible quotations are from the King James Version of
The Holy Bible, unless otherwise marked.

First printing, August 1986

Library of Congress Catalog Card Number 86-50200
ISBN 0-8423-7146-X
Copyright 1986 by Valetta Steel
Printed in the United States of America

CONTENTS

CONTENTS

ONE

The Valley's Approach

Looking back on that day—I struggle to remember just how it was.

It began as any other winter day, the smoky February sun gradually illuminating, but hardly warming, the lifeless landscape. As I sat down to the breakfast table, out of the corner of my eye I watched Lorna, my fifteen-year-old daughter, impatiently pulling a comb through her long blonde tresses.

She threw a maroon coat over her small shoulders. "Bye, Mom," she shouted and hurried out the door in pursuit of the school bus. It was Friday.

Mid-morning and still nothing to distinguish this day from a hundred others. At my desk in the missions office where I worked, I wrestled with the news release that would be due on Monday morning.

The phone rang. It was Leon, my seventeen-year-old son, who was happily working through his freshman year of college at Greenville, Illinois.

"Mom," he began excitedly, "can you pick me up this afternoon? Our concert has been scratched. It would be great if I could come home."

"Sure, Leon," I answered. His deep maturing voice sent a warm glow through me. Now that he was older, bursting with ideas and dreams, talkative and challenging, taking his father's place as the man of the family, there was a rich and growing bond between us.

"It'd be great to have you home for the weekend. What time should I come?"

Three weeks earlier, Leon had jammed clothing and an accumulation of his most prized belongings into a couple of suitcases and headed for Greenville, a church school on the flat, featureless plains of southern Illinois.

Still seventeen, he had finished high school at mid-year, graduating with honors. Through the summer he had seemed like a thoroughbred at the starting gate, impatiently pawing the track. "College will be super," he confided. "I just know it."

His first call home brought news that he had been asked to join a campus musical group.

"They're called *The Re-Created*," he explained. "Neat kids. It's really an honor to be invited. We'll be out weekends sharing Christ."

I left my office at noon. Sliding behind the wheel of my blue Montego, I eased out into the traffic flowing along Highway 31 toward the heart of Indianapolis, past the suburban landmarks familiar to a thousand communities—a local shopping mall, Sears, Ponderosa, Burger King.

Off the beltline, I soon was on Interstate 70 heading west. The highway stretched before me like a broad gray divider, intersecting acres of corn fields and a succession of siloed Indiana towns that magically stir to life every Friday night when Indiana basketball fever takes over.

It was mid-afternoon and getting colder when I pulled off the interstate into the sleepy village of Greenville, its substantial brick homes and well-ordered streets inevitably leading to the campus of Greenville College.

Turning into the parking lot, I switched off the ignition and paused, wondering where to begin my search for Leon. Then, before I could open the door, Leon appeared as if from nowhere. As I looked up at his six-foot frame, I felt a surge of pride. The wide smile showed a row of evenly spaced white teeth. Gentle blue eyes. I noted a struggling new moustache.

"Mom, come on up and see my room," he began, "and you've got to meet some of my profs. We've even planned a dorm tea for you. And, Mom, there is something else I've done. I hope it will be OK."

"Like what?"

"Well, I've invited Don, the leader of our musical group, home for the weekend. Is that OK?"

By the time we left Greenville, we had acquired three more passengers, students needing rides home to Indianapolis.

"Mom, how about letting me drive?" Leon asked.

"Well, OK," I said, "but be careful. It's starting to rain." Leon had had his driver's license a year and had shown himself a good driver. I slid over and let him take the wheel. As we approached Indianapolis, the interstate clotted with weekend traffic, and in the deepening twilight taillights bled pools of red across the highway ahead of us. It was getting colder. The snow tires hummed noisily, and windshield wipers thumped their steady beat, almost in rhythm with the pattering rain.

"Please, be careful, Leon," I found myself saying as I watched the water glisten like ice on the fences we passed.

Indianapolis cast a dome of light against the low cloud ceiling. On the outskirts we unloaded our passengers in the cold rain, and then we headed south into the suburb of Greenwood. We could see the distinctive grillwork of the "ORMISO HEIGHTS" sign, marking the entrance to the headquarter complex of OMS International where I worked and lived. In a moment our big white apartment building appeared in the headlights, smiling a bright welcome.

"Leon, you're home!" Lorna squealed as she flung open the front door. Suddenly she looked older than her fifteen years. With fair skin and honey-blonde hair, she was a striking contrast to her dark-complexioned brother, who towered a full foot above her.

When Leon introduced his friend, Don, as our weekend guest, I detected distress signals coming from Lorna. In a moment she tugged at my sleeve and eased me into the kitchen.

"Mom," she wailed, "you didn't tell me we were having company. I don't know if I've fixed enough food. What'll I do?"

"It's OK, honey," I soothed. "There'll be plenty. I don't eat much."

Lorna placed her creation, a dish of Indian curry, on the table, along with a salad and vegetables. We sat down, bowed our heads for grace, and began eating.

Lorna shot a glance at her brother who was cautiously sampling her new dish.

"You don't like it," she accused. "I can tell you don't like it."

"No, no. Honestly I do. It's really good."

"No," she insisted, "I can tell. You really don't like it."

The conversation had a comfortable and familiar ring to it. It felt good to have Leon home.

Dinner over, Leon announced that he and Don would drive over to see Leon's girl-friend, Wynoka.

"Hey, Lorna. How about coming along?"

Now that was something. Inviting his kid sister! College was making a real gentleman of Leon, I decided.

"Don't worry, Mom," Leon called out. "We'll just bowl a game or two and be back early. Won't be long."

As the car moved away into the darkness, I noted that it was still raining, but now it seemed colder. Temperatures were dropping sharply.

It seems somehow incongruous that the days which irrevocably change one's life on earth should be filled with ordinary events: the rising of an ordinary February sun, an office filled with ordinary conversations, the sound of telephones ringing and car doors slamming and friendly *hello's* and dull rain and, "Leon, I know you really don't like it!"

No, looking back and reliving those final precious moments of earthly time, it still seems wrong that the valley should approach that way. There should be intimations and gentle cautions.

Half an hour later the doorbell summoned me to the front door to look wonderingly into the face of a blue-uniformed police officer.

"Are you Mrs. Steel?" he began slowly, as though groping for the right words. Or was this a speech he had given before, the words nearly memorized? I cannot be sure.

"Yes, I'm Mrs. Steel."

"Mrs. Steel, do you have a teenage boy about eighteen and a girl a little younger?"

"Well, yes, I do," I mumbled.

"Mrs. Steel, it's getting colder. The rain is turning to ice. There has just been an accident on the 37 bypass. I'm sorry to have to tell you that your children and their friend have just been killed."

Suddenly I felt as if I had been pushed over a high cliff into a wild seething sea unable to swim. My mind was creating images: Leon and Lorna in their final moment, as the car spun out of control, and then the crunch of metal against their soft flesh. *It was too much.* The accident which had taken their lives would now surely take mine as well.

But at that very moment, I felt myself in the strong embrace of the Spirit of God. I was being lifted upward, above the cold winter trees, sweetly, securely, into the warm presence of my Father. With a calm, which I instinctively knew had its source from beyond my own being, I heard myself saying, "Officer, I know where they are. They are with God."

Now there would be the phone calls, consoling friends, flowers, "arrangements," and at last the long caravan of cars heading to the familiar plot of ground and newly spaded earth. Here I was walking the valley again—a painful scenario I knew too well. And yet concurrently, in the dark countenance of death, there kept coming sweet tokens from my mighty and loving heavenly Father. His love came in great billows, washing over my broken and bleeding heart, bringing again that refreshing comfort to me.

"Yea, though I walk through the valley of the shadow of death, I will fear no evil: for thou art with me" (Ps. 23:4). Yes, this was the valley again. I recognized it all right. It comes on you suddenly with a phone call, a knock at the door, the appearance of the messenger, and the word. The first time the word had been "leukemia."

T W O

Lessons from the Alchemy of Suffering

He was born September 2, 1952, and we named him Daniel Phillip. I was nineteen when Danny was born. Henry and I had been married a little over a year. When expectant mothers fabricate dreams of their firstborn, mentally creating the child they hope for, I would guess that half the women in America would conjure up a child like Danny.

A chubby little guy, he arrived with a head of blond hair, huge blue eyes, and a personality that would charm a cobra. Happy and content with the world, he was usually brimming with laughter, a friend to every creature that came across his path.

By the time he was two, our hometown, Sherwood, Michigan, had adopted Danny as the unofficial town mascot. He was a familiar sight on Main Street of the little village, a big cowboy hat pushed down over his head and a pair of six-guns dangling from his hips. Almost any weekday morning he could be seen sauntering alongside his daddy on their morning trip to the post office. He knew scores of the town folk by name. He greeted strangers and friends alike with a wide grin and childish chatter. "Hi, ya, Mr. Frank," he would call out.

"Hi, ya, Danny. How's the old *Lone Ranger* doing this morning?"

Looking with eyes full of wonder and awe at our firstborn, Henry had reverently spoken the words, "My son"—words that he had seldom heard from the lips of his own father, except in anger or displeasure. I, too, longed to be the warm and loving mother I had never known.

Not that my mother had been a harsh or unkind person, but she had grown up in hard times and in a family where feelings and conflicts were deeply buried. There was little time for laughter or play. Driving along Route 41, just outside Lowell, south of Gary, I can still reflect upon a rusted old windmill, the forlorn landmark on the edge of the Haberlin place, a 200-acre farm that had been in Mother's family for three generations, and on which her forebears struggled daily to eke out a modest living. Those were hard times. My parents had eloped in 1930, and I was born three years later in the depths of the Great Depression.

I am sure that in her way Mother had loved us. "I love you," however, was an expression no one ever heard escape her lips. She was not one given to displays of affection, and when Dad would put his burly arms around her slender figure, she would pull away in embarrassment.

Children had come in relentless succession. I arrived two years after Arthur, then came Leonora, my dearest friend and confidant; we were followed by Eugene, Ronnie, Sharon, and Melvin.

School-day mornings at the Stevenson house seemed a nerve-wracking exercise in which Mother, increasingly distraught and furrowed of brow, orchestrated a tense drama designed to move a houseful of wriggling youngsters through a routine of dressing, chores, breakfast, and finally onto the school bus. The approaching bus loomed in her mind as a kind of doomsday machine, perversely designed to prove her an incompetent mother. Each morning featured some small trauma, and repeatedly I climbed exhausted onto the yellow school bus.

All her life Mother seemed to struggle frantically to keep her world under control. While occasionally recalling her dream of becoming a schoolteacher, she set her mind dutifully to cook three meals a day and labor hours over what seemed to be tons of laundry. The drudgery of it had turned her face into a dour mask of anxiety and joylessness.

By the time I was sixteen, I found myself yearning to get away from home. Mother's burdens were becoming my burdens, and they seemed too heavy. I also felt inhibited and stifled with a mother I could neither talk to nor understand, and from whom I felt no affection. I dreamed of doing something for God with my life and wondered who could help me.

But if Mother's personality seemed cold and distant, I found my father's a harbor of warmth and security in the troubled ocean of my growing-up years. By no means perfect, he could be narrow-minded and strict. Yet he possessed a deep devotion to God, a wholesome enthusiasm for life, and unshakable integrity. Everyone who knew him admired him.

Yet, at heart, Dad was a nomad, and he came by his wandering ways naturally. His own father, an original Michigan hillbilly, had come from an unruly gypsy-like clan that never stayed anywhere long enough to put down roots. In the process of acquiring a grade-school education, Dad had enrolled in fifteen schools. He passed down to us lurid tales of hunting dogs and porcupines and wild exploits of the Stevensons. "That Stevenson bunch," someone remarked in later years, "if they don't get religion, they'll end up boozers!"

With the Depression beginning, Dad had been invited to Indiana by his sister, who had married a young pastor, Lester Lee, and there he met my mother in a home prayer meeting. They married and then moved to Toledo, Ohio, where Dad set about to look for work: a bleak prospect in 1930. When someone mentioned that the Auto-Lite Company was hiring, he hurried to the employment office, only to discover a line of a hundred other desperate and hopeful applicants. But by seven-thirty that evening, with no prospect of a job in sight, all but two of the applicants had gone home. Both were hired, and Dad was one of them.

At Auto-Lite he proved himself an able and reliable worker, gradually helping pay off the mountain of debts his father had accumulated, while building a small home for Mother and himself. He was amazed at his wife's ability to save money, something unheard of in his family. But as the unions strong-armed their way into the shop, pressuring all the workers to join, something in Dad revolted.

He wanted no part in the union's methods, in their drinking parties and vulgar language. Despite remonstrances of friends, Dad would not budge. Never one to make speeches, when it came to matters of conscience, he was a man of unshakable convictions and unyielding scruples. As a result, he was blacklisted by the union and many times passed over for promotions.

When I was seven we moved to a small, 22-acre farm near Temperance, Michigan. Dad enlarged and remodeled our farmhouse to accommodate our ever-increasing clan. The back porch was enclosed to provide living quarters for my grandmother, who lived with us periodically until her death.

Following the construction of our farmhouse, Dad began building other houses and eventually obtained a contractor's license.

Dad could be tough. There were no cash allowances for the Stevenson kids. We earned every cent, and the use of the family automobile was carefully allocated. Yet, to an amazing degree, Dad gave us free reign. Though I doubt that he had ever read a book on child psychology, he was a genius at instilling in us healthy motivation. He taught us a wholesome fear of God, so much so that he seldom had to resort to his own disciplinary measures.

He taught by example. Today, all seven children live productive Christian lives. Two of us, my sister Lea and I, are missionaries, and brothers Eugene and Melvin are ministers.

Dad often appeared happy and easy-going, but resisting his authority meant swift and certain retribution. I learned this for myself one summer afternoon in the potato patch behind the barn. Tired and disenchanted from grovelling around in the dirt for potatoes, a family project, I wandered off to amuse myself in other ways. When Dad ordered me back on the job, I clearly indicated I had other ideas. He stood up abruptly, strode over to a nearby tree, and fashioned a switch. Sensing doom, I scurried back into the patch and started digging with fervor. It was a lesson not lost on me. Children find security in tough parents who express clear demands and then enforce them.

But above all, Dad's faith and love proved to be the rudder of my young life. During his own teenage years, when his family lived in Toledo, he was invited to a revival in a small church where sinners were customarily invited to kneel at the altar to "get right with God." At the invitation he longed to go forward, but shy and timid, he hung back. Finally, someone offered to accompany him, and that night Dad asked Christ into his life. "As I walked home that night," he loved to recount, "the stars were brighter, crisper. I felt a peace I had never known. Even the trees seemed to be singing."

When he told his family what he had done, the response was predictable. "George's got religion," they guffawed. But there was no gainsaying; a radical change had taken place in his life. He had indeed been born again. Later both parents, his sisters, and three brothers came to Christ.

Dad joined the local church and became a faithful member of the sort that were referred to as "pillars" of the congregation. Family devotions were a regular regimen in our home. Every night after supper, Dad would get out the big, leather-bound, well-thumbed Bible. Then, one by one, each of us would pray, and Dad would lead us in the Lord's Prayer. Dad always prayed in conversational tones, as though on uncomplicated terms with his Lord.

When I reached my twelfth year, there came a growing conviction that I should give myself to God. The moment arrived, not in a church service, but in the quiet of my room. I eased myself down onto the linoleum floor by my bed, confessed every sin I could remember, and asked Jesus into my heart. I was surprised not to feel a rush of emotion as I had expected. In fact, it was nothing like Dad's conversion experience, a fact that troubled me with doubt for years to come.

Was I a Christian? I hoped so. I loved the Lord and had done all I knew to do, and yet I wished I could talk about it with someone, maybe my mother. But she had a faith of her own. I am sure it was a real faith, and yet she never spoke of it. Even her prayers in public were soft, timid utterances as though she were fearful someone might hear and raise a question, or peer disapprovingly into her soul.

But there were things Mother could talk about easily and one of them was saving money. Saving money had been a way of life. Like many Americans who had had to scrounge and scrimp through the Depression years, she never spent a penny unnecessarily. As for clothes, why should anyone need more than a few dresses? she would ask. Something to cover the body and provide reasonable modesty would suffice. After all, as she had often informed me, she had had only two dresses as a girl.

The issue of clothes was a sore spot with me. It was not simply that I felt I needed more and better clothes. What bothered me was that I was often forced to wear garments quite unlike anything worn by anyone else in my class—long brown stockings, for instance.

"Let's not see any more bare legs around here," Dad admonished.

"But, Dad," I protested tearfully, "no one else in my school wears these awful old stockings. I hate them."

"Yes, but it is winter, and they're good for you."

"But," I wailed, "how would you like to go to work in black silk trousers when everyone else was wearing overalls?"

Apparently my logic, or my tears, were not lost on him, and he proved more understanding than I had given him credit for. Yet my narrow, provincial environment, combined with my emotional estrangement from my mother, seemed increasingly discouraging.

I longed to escape, to go away to school. So during my freshman year, when a youth choir from a small Christian high school and junior college came to our church, I seized the occasion to make my case. "Dad," I said, "I want to go to Spring Arbor to school. I really do." Astonishingly, Mother did not object, and Dad seemed almost pleased. Perhaps it was because his older sister, Dorothy, had graduated from the same school and married a minister.

Thus, my sophomore year found me in a Christian high school in Spring Arbor, Michigan. It was there that I met Henry Steel, a skinny, awkward youth. He could be loud and brash, yet he exuded charm, and his air of self-confidence, reminiscent of my dad's, attracted me to him.

Henry was a senior. Three years later, after I had finished a year of college, and Henry had graduated from junior college, we were married.

With our financial resources exhausted, and no prospect of help from either of our families, we decided to move to Temperance, work, and save money for a year so Henry could continue college. We purchased a small trailer.

I found a secretarial job at a plant in Toledo which manufactured atomizers. Henry worked at Willy's Overland and assisted Dad in contracting. At the same time he served as youth minister in my home church, now pastored by a dynamic young man, Larry Burr, who was to play a key role in the future course of our lives.

Early the next year I discovered I was

pregnant. As summer came the conference superintendent asked Henry to take the pastorate of a small church in Sherwood, Michigan. After much prayer Henry accepted. For the present, at least, his college degree would have to wait.

It was September when Henry first drove me to Sherwood. The little town, midway between Battle Creek and Jackson, had once been a thriving industrial center, boasting numerous factories, a high school, a railway station, even a college. But Sherwood, failing to keep pace with changing times, had dwindled into a sleepy village. Huge oak trees, heavy with leaves, draped the quiet neighborhood. We drove past an old gentleman shuffling slowly along the all-but-deserted Main Street. He seemed somehow to symbolize that half-forgotten hamlet, old and weary and having no place to go.

Two church buildings fronted on Main Street. The larger of the two, the Methodist Church, had long since been closed. Its dilapidated steeple now sheltered a small flock of pigeons. Across the street stood the smaller Free Methodist Church, a building distinguished by two small front doors which were reminiscent of old Shaker dwellings. This was the church to which we had been appointed. It was, in fact, the oldest building of our denomination in

Michigan. Conference leaders had been proposing that the church be disbanded and the building turned into a museum.

Henry drove past the church to the edge of town and turned into a narrow drive that led to a shabby house. "This is it," he announced without emotion. "Our new home." I slowly surveyed the lumpy shingles, broken windows, the tangle of weeds that edged up against the front steps. I felt a lump rising in my throat. "Really? Henry," I whispered, "is this it?"

There was a long pause, and then he grinned impishly and started the car. On down the street he turned into a driveway. There stood a frame house with a flat wood porch, but this house was newly painted with windows that glistened. Even the lawn was freshly mowed. Still sputtering, I hardly noticed how old it was. Already it had a "homey" feel to it.

Danny was born on September 2, and ten days later we moved into the Sherwood parsonage. The money we had saved for college went into furnishing the house. We rummaged through second-hand stores until we found living room furniture consisting of a huge, red velvet couch and some faded, overstuffed chairs. An ancient, well-scarred table went into the dining room. After buying beds, there was just enough money left for a washing machine and refrigerator.

The Sunday morning offering, our salary, rarely exceeded $40. Here was a chance for us to prove Matthew 6:33: "Seek first his kingdom and his righteousness, and all these things will be given to you as well" (NIV). If we would really seek first the kingdom of God, his promise was that "these things" would be added unto us, and there were plenty of "these things."

The expenses piled up. The baby needed diapers and an increasing supply of baby food to satisfy his growing appetite. Then came heating fuel, gasoline, tires, car payments, insurance premiums, to say nothing of groceries. Usually, by the time the weekend arrived, we were totally insolvent.

But repeatedly God provided. Sometimes it would be an anonymous offering slipped into our mailbox, or the fee from a wedding or funeral. Church people would appear at the door unannounced with a basket of produce, a package of beef, or some chickens.

As the congregation grew, the board fashioned a budget. Our salary was increased and a car allowance was paid for visitation and church work. From our hearts we sang, "Praise God from whom all blessings flow."

Meanwhile, the little Sherwood church was experiencing a resurrection of such magnitude that church leaders all over the state were taking notice. The original congregation of twenty-five to thirty had doubled and doubled and doubled again. Henry and I dreamed of dozens of schemes to increase church attendance, and to each of them Henry brought his soaring vitality.

No one in Sherwood could remember anything quite like it. People who had previously shown no interest in religion came out of curiosity to observe the phenomenon. Tirelessly, we worked with young people, began Sunday school training seminars, planned Sunday school promotions, and organized a quiz team that took second place in the state finals.

Together we spent hours brainstorming on how to use the talents of each person who came to the church. The people kept coming. Chairs were put in the aisles to accommodate the overflow. When Sunday morning attendance reached a hundred and fifty in the little church, it was clear something had to be done. And, as usual, Henry and I began dreaming up ideas.

Although the old Methodist Church across the street had been condemned as a fire hazard, Henry learned that it was not beyond repair. He made an offer to the denomination of $1,000, which the leadership promptly accepted. Renovation would cost a little more—about $6,000—and Henry erected a huge thermometer in front of the church to chart the progress of the building fund. His slogan was "Build for Tomorrow."

Gradually the old building underwent a remarkable transformation. Volunteers came to wield a paint brush, a hammer, wash windows, scrub floors, or pull weeds. The women and I prepared potluck dinners on the lawn. My father, an experienced builder, helped rebuild the crumbling belfry. The pigeons would have to find a new home.

As the work progressed in Sherwood, we agreed that Henry should get on with his schooling. This meant additional expenses plus the cost of commuting fifty miles several days a week to Spring Arbor. There seemed only one way to make ends meet: I would have to work. I found a job as a secretary in the Douglas Manufacturing plant in nearby Bronson. This meant leaving Danny each morning in the care of his "grand-mothers," church women who offered to care for him while I worked.

As I pulled in front of Mrs. Masters' or Mrs. Myers' home each morning, the first rays of sun would just begin to touch the sky with orange and pink. "Good-bye, Danny. Be a good boy. I love you."

Backing out of the drive I could hear his

laughter. I held back the tears as I drove away. Often, as I was punching at the typewriter, my thoughts flitted to Henry, to the church, to a dozen activities that required my attention, to meals that needed planning, and then to Danny, my precious Danny, not yet a year old. What kind of mother was I? Other women were raising my child. But this was only a temporary arrangement, I consoled myself. Before too long Henry would have his degree, and I would be home with Danny. Life would slow down and settle into a comfortable, manageable routine.

I was approaching my twentieth birthday, the age when most girls are enjoying the full bloom of youthful energy. But I was exhausted, stretched to the breaking point, trying just to keep pace with my dynamo of a husband and my own ambitious ideals. "Lord," I would pray, "just give me strength to get through one more day."

Weekends, instead of providing some rest from my demanding schedule, usually meant an even more frenzied pace. The parsonage seemed to be a continuous open house, a hub of ceaseless activity. This was the way I had always wanted my home to be, but now I was tired, so tired, and there seemed never enough time to do what needed to be done.

I remember one Saturday morning after mopping floors, straightening the house, doing the week's wash, and finding a few moments to play with Danny—just savoring being at home for a change—I flopped down on the sofa, totally spent. With lunch hardly over, one of the church members dropped in, bringing with him a big apple pie.

People seldom stopped by the Steel parsonage for only a minute. Henry was a good listener, a brilliant conversationalist with a flair for entertaining people. The bearer of the pie was hardly out the door when a delegation of men involved in the prison ministry appeared for fellowship. Now the phone was ringing—it was our new director of music calling to ask if it was all right for him to eat dinner with us.

By nine-thirty that evening I was still in the kitchen finishing the last of the supper dishes when Henry poked his head in.

"Valetta," he asked, "could you type up my sermon outline and give me some feedback?"

"I can't. I just can't," I pleaded. "I still have the bulletin to do and the hymns need to be chosen."

It was eleven-thirty when I finished the stencil and began cranking the old mimeograph machine. The ink was cold and blotched. I noticed a misspelled word and decided to ignore it. Finally I tumbled into bed, but it seemed only moments until the alarm rang, prodding me up and into another day of ceaseless demands.

About five minutes before church Henry glanced at the bulletin.

"Valetta," he snapped, "there is a big mistake here. How could you let this happen?"

The dyke of my emotional control and spiritual serenity broke.

"OK, OK," I shot back. "You can do it yourself if all you are ever going to do is criticize."

As soon as I had spoken those words, I regretted them and wished desperately I could somehow snatch them back. What had happened to the inward poise in which I took such pride? I was growing touchy and irritable. Almost every day, it seemed, I had to ask God and others to forgive me for my attitude.

Henry's counsel too often seemed like preaching to me. Why couldn't he meet my needs? Why wasn't he sensitive to my hurts, to my weariness? I had given him my life, my future, my dreams, and now when I needed him most, he didn't understand. Somehow he couldn't help me. Did he really care?

"You don't love me," I shouted one day.

"Why can't you understand and help me rather than preach at me?"

My words brought a look of stunned disbelief. "Of course I love you," he said in a voice that seemed suddenly low and pained. "I can't imagine a day without you. For you to even think that hurts and disappoints me. Valetta, sometimes I just don't understand you."

Gradually the Lord revealed to me that a great deal of the pressure and anxiety I was feeling was the result of a vain and hopeless effort to conform to the role of "model wife"—a standard I imagined my gifted husband demanded of me. One morning, as I waited on my knees with my Bible open, the Lord spoke to me through the Psalms. "It is better to trust in the Lord than to put confidence in man" (Ps. 118:8). God showed me that I had made an idol of my husband. Now, in the light of God's Word, I saw Henry as a man: handsome, responsible, caring, demanding, and yet not perfect, not all-knowing, not all-powerful. I must put my ultimate trust in God and not in man. It was a lesson I was just beginning to learn, and would have to learn in a far deeper way in the months and years ahead.

Still, life moved on at a relentless pace, and for Henry there was no letting up. Every success surged him on to greater challenges. He purchased a second-hand printing press, rented a vacant bank building in town, and set up a print shop. It was not enough that Henry Steel was a student, minister, pastor, youth leader, church builder, baseball player, to say nothing of father and husband; he now aspired to head a small publishing enterprise.

While the congregation responded with mounting enthusiasm to the vision and charisma of this young man, his wife was foundering along in his wake, somehow trying to establish order in the turmoil of life. I seemed to be climbing a steep mountain, but I told myself, "Once I reach the summit, the going will be easier—it will be downhill from there. There will be times to relax and lead a normal life." And then one day that winter I realized, with a curious mixture of joy and dread, that I was pregnant again.

I quit my job in Bronson, and our second son was born October 19. Dark in complexion, he bore a striking resemblance to his father. "Let's name him Henry," I suggested. "Oh, no, you don't," my husband protested. "We are not going to saddle the kid with a name like Henry." Finally we arrived at a compromise. He would be called Leon Henry. For me, having another baby meant back to the nursery, to the routine of handling diapers. But I found some degree of comfort in all this. Life would actually be simpler for me as fewer demands are made of new mothers. Two years and one month separated Danny and Leon. Danny would have a playmate and Leon a big brother to initiate him into the mysteries and adventures of boyhood.

The small earthquake that was taking place in Sherwood had not failed to attract the attention of our church leadership. Moreover, Henry was rapidly gaining a reputation as one of the most exciting young preachers in the denomination. It was no surprise when a phone call from church headquarters came one evening inviting Henry to be official youth delegate at the general conference. This would be a good time, I told myself, to get away for a few days. I would take Danny and Leon to visit my parents in Temperance.

When I returned home though, I noticed that Danny seemed irritable, crotchety; he seemed to be in discomfort. He would start crying for no reason. One morning as I glanced out a kitchen window, I noticed him struggling with his tricycle. He seemed to have difficulty manipulating the handlebars. "Mommy," he cried out, "my arm hurts."

Putting the children in the car, I drove to

nearby Coldwater to consult the doctor. After examining Danny, Dr. Mooi, a family friend, looked puzzled. "I am afraid there may be something wrong with the bone," he said. "I'd like to do a biopsy tomorrow." When I got home I called Henry, and he returned home that same evening. "I shared our concern for Danny with the whole conference," he told me. "They are all praying for us."

When we arrived at the hospital the next morning we were directed down a long hall to a small emergency center. A blood test would precede the biopsy. Danny screamed as the nurse pricked his finger with a scalpel and caused blood to spurt. Then we waited for hours, it seemed.

Finally Dr. Mooi appeared, beckoning us into his office. "We are canceling the biopsy because we believe we have already diagnosed the problem," he said. Then, slowly and in measured, professional tones, he went on. "The white blood count is very high, and we suspect that your son has acute lymphatic leukemia. However, we are hoping our diagnosis is wrong, and we would like you to take Danny to Ann Arbor University Hospital."

There was a long, awkward pause, then in a voice, gentle and subdued, Dr. Mooi continued. "Telling you this is one of the hardest things I have ever had to do. We don't know why many children from good homes develop this disease. Unfortunately, it is not curable at this time. All we can do is offer you treatments which could extend his time to five or six months, maybe more." His voice trailed off. "Or maybe we'll find a cure."

We sat there stunned, struggling to take in the import of what Dr. Mooi had said. And yet, at the same time, we somehow wanted to erase the whole conversation from our consciousnesses. Surely these words had not been spoken to *us*. He was speaking about someone else, not *our* son, not Danny. These things happen only to other people in faraway places: people you read about in newspapers, strangers or perhaps even people in the church, but not to you.

Leukemia. The word was familiar enough to me. I had read it many times in magazines and books. Those who have known its victims speak the word in hushed tones, freighted with pity or horror. This was the blood disease without a cure. Increasing debility leading to a slow, painful death: that was leukemia. But it was a disease that happened to other people.

As we climbed into our old Ford and drove to Ann Arbor, there remained a lingering thread of hope. The doctor had not been absolutely certain of his diagnosis. That was the whole point of this trip; that was why we were going to Ann Arbor. Doctors are often mistaken. It happens every day. There was a chance, possibly a good chance, that the whole diagnosis was a big mistake. In a few hours we would awaken from this nightmare and drive home with Danny between us, praising the Lord it was all over.

When we arrived in the parking lot in Ann Arbor, we walked into a huge octopus-like building with its many wings stretching out like tentacles in every direction. We were directed to a spacious waiting room, alive with color, obviously designed and decorated for children. Scattered about were toys and Dr. Seuss books on under-sized tables.

The room was full of youngsters, most of them apparently normal. I soon learned, however, that they too were on death's row, under the sentence of that terrible disease.

In the examining room the nurse reached for Danny's finger and made a quick incision. Danny screamed, and each childish wail found an echo in my own wounded spirit and brought a huge lump to my throat. *We will love him so much and take such good care of him*, I thought. *Certainly he will be different. He will get well. We'll find the best physicians in the world, and, of course, God will help.* Soon enough we got the report which only confirmed Dr. Mooi's diagnosis—leukemia. Apart from a miracle, Danny had no more than a few months to live.

I've tried many times to analyze the phenomenon—how a single moment, a single word, can forever alter the shape of one's world. The mind struggles to comprehend, yet it revolts. The heart will not accept what reason insists is fact. Then, slowly, at intervals, the facts begin to seep down from the numbed brain into the heart, bringing a kind of paralysis. At the same time comes a vague, nagging sense of guilt. Why me? Why us? are the questions that intrude again and again. Where did we fail? Was there something we could have done that we didn't do? Is God punishing us?

When we returned home bearing in our arms our firstborn, who was now under the sentence of death, something happened that illustrated the tremendous courage and unselfishness of my husband. As we pulled into Sherwood, Henry clapped his hand to his forehead and said, "Valetta, the baseball game tonight! I forgot all about it, and we have the equipment in the trunk of the car." At the field, we found the team waiting. When they heard the tragic diagnosis, it was suggested that the game be called off.

"Called off?" echoed Henry. "I should say not. We'll go right ahead and play it, and since I'm your star player, don't tell me I shouldn't play either." He did play. It was typical of Henry, never allowing his personal sorrow to cast a shadow upon the joy of another. He looked upon burdening others with his pain as selfishness.

Though Danny was now very sick, the doctors agreed it would be best for him to stay home and be cared for as an outpatient, returning to the hospital every two weeks for observation and treatment. As we traveled the long miles back and forth to the Ann Arbor hospital, leaving Leon behind in the care of Grandmother Myers, the old Ford became for us a kind of sanctuary. God in the presence of the Holy Spirit was with us in a very precious way.

We comforted one another with our recent gleanings from the Word, insights God had given us into the meaning of life and death. Up to this point death had seemed always remote, a transition relegated to the distant future. This was our first trip through the valley. Someone has said that life is always seen most clearly in the face of death. It is true. In that dark valley the shadows show more perfectly the true arrangement of life's terrain, the substance of reality.

In the weeks that followed we kept constant vigil over our stricken child. Was he in pain? Was he losing weight? "Danny will have no resistance to infection," the doctors had warned us. Antibiotics would help only temporarily, and, above all, he had to be kept from catching colds and the flu. Danny came to understand and accept without self-pity his condition, and his spirit touched us deeply.

The only time he did not cooperate was when the nurses approached for the routine blood tests. "I don't want you to take my blood," he would scream, and my heart ached to spare him the ordeal. At times he would look at me with solemn eyes, now bigger than ever against his paling skin. "When will I get well, Mommy?" he would ask. And I would turn away in silence. I had no words to formulate an answer.

We set up a bed for Danny in the dining room, and this big room, which had so recently been the command center for Henry's plethora of church activities, now took on the appearance of a hospital room. We had begun a solemn countdown of days that would bring us to the last fleeting moments of this precious life that had brought us so much sunshine. That shine was fading away. Yet overshadowing those days was the Heavenly Presence, gently infusing us with the mysterious hope that is the birthright of every believer: resurrection. That doctrine to which we had always paid lip service was now coming clear.

It is the curious nature of leukemia and other forms of cancer to periodically go into remission. For a time Danny responded to therapy. Some of his energy returned, bringing with it a wistful, wild hope that maybe the diagnosis had been wrong. Or was God answering our prayers with a divine miracle of healing? It seemed too much to hope for. One afternoon after his nap, I watched Danny struggle to pull himself erect in his crib. Turning a bright face to me, he cried, "Mommy, see, I'm getting better."

"Danny," I whispered to comfort myself as much as him, "Jesus loves you very much, and he will always be with you."

When the remissions came, providing a brief reprieve from the relentless march of the disease, a slight recovery of strength would come to Danny. These were golden hours we savored to the fullest. I would strap on Danny's six-guns, find the battered cowboy hat, and soon it would be time for cowboys and Indians again. Henry had bought him an oversized plastic bat. The two of them would tumble out on the lawn for "baseball." As I stood watching from the window, their shouts and laughter came to my ears with a terrible sweetness.

We were learning something new about the preciousness of time. With the doctor's words, "a few months," we had begun mentally to tick off the days. We could no longer think of Danny's life, our time together with him, as stretching out into a distant future. We could no longer project in our minds' eyes scenes of childhood, teenage years, college, adulthood. In a moment, our perspective had changed. Time now was seen as a priceless commodity, so fragile and fleeting. How important that we treasure every hour with our son.

It was as though the joys of a normal life span were being distilled and poured into a few dwindling golden days. Thus, strange as it may seem, those last months were studded with good times, laughter, and fun. When Danny was able to respond, how willingly I would drop everything. I would think, *I can't let this opportunity pass.*

Gradually, I began to understand that this is the way one should view every moment, every day of his life, as an infinitely precious commodity. How often in our frenzied plans for the future are we too busy for the present? As I study the life of our Lord, I am impressed that there was about him, as one writer puts it, a certain "large sense of leisure." He had time for people. When he saw that people needed him, he zeroed in on them, giving of himself without worrying about time.

Parents often wish they had learned Christ's example when their children were growing up: during those tumultuous teenage years when eternal moments were passing. But they were busy with a hundred other things, and now they look back with regret on hours, days, and years that cannot be recovered.

For us, the good times stood out in bold relief—bright jewels against the dark background of pain and weakness. Each remission inevitably was followed by a fresh onslaught of the malignancy, so irrevocably entrenched in our oldest son's little body. While Leon thrived, Danny wasted away. Pale and quiet, he lay on his bed and turned large pitiful eyes to us in silent pleas for help. His small face grew puffed, and his skin took on a shiny appearance. His stomach became extended. A painful urinary infection developed that strong medication could not cure. It seemed we were continually making fruitless trips with Danny to the hospital.

The disease often would produce a tremendous thirst that nothing seemed to quench. Through long night hours I would often sit weeping and praying with Danny on my lap. One night I cried to God, "Lord, was it like this at Calvary?" Then I thought, *You went through it for me, so surely you must love me and understand my pain.*

When Christians go through experiences like this one, we expect ourselves to remember all the sermons we have ever heard on the meaning of suffering, and recall all the books we have read explaining God's providential ways. We are to appreciate that through these strange circumstances that make up the fiery ordeal, there is a purging, a stretching, an enriching. All of these things are taking place, of course. A day came when I could look back and say, "Yes, Lord. Thank you. I can see your purposes now. I think I can understand at least a part of the meaning of it all."

But I have to be honest in saying that as we sat there through those long night hours, trying to quench our son's unquenchable thirst, trying to soothe and bring relief; when I stood at my kitchen sink, my hands in dishwater, my tormented heart lifted to God with salty tears running down my cheeks—I wasn't seeing the full picture. What I was doing was asking God for his strength, his grace, just for that moment, that hour, to get me through that day.

I began to grasp an important fact. God does not ask us to bear the whole burden at once. He asks only that we live through that moment, that hour, that day, and his promise is that "as thy days, so shall thy strength be" (Deut. 3:25). I learned not to ask God for big, earth-shaking events. I would think, *Here is our little Sherwood community, and these people are praying for me; praying that somehow I'll get through this ordeal and that I'll be a witness for Christ. Lord, don't let me let you down.*

Later, someone asked me if there ever was a time when I thought I just couldn't take it anymore. I could honestly answer, "No." My reason was simple.

Psalm 1 describes the person who is "like a tree planted by rivers of water." Not only does he "bringeth forth his fruit in his season" but "his leaf also shall not wither." The Psalmist tells us that this person meditates upon the Word of God, day and night.

A nice picture. During the trying times with Danny, I was discovering in my life this profound truth: that meditating on the Word of God had made me strong—like the Psalmist's tree. As a teenager I had tried to imitate my father and his love for the Bible. When I went away to school at Spring Arbor, I had determined that no matter how busy my daily schedule became, nothing would crowd out my time alone with the Lord. Though I occasionally missed my devotions, God enabled me for the most part to keep my pledge to end each day in the Word with him.

It was never my habit to read long passages of Scripture at one time, but rather to take shorter portions, meditate upon them, turn them over and over in my mind. The Holy Spirit seemed to guide me to certain passages which became precious favorites. I marked verses that seemed to apply to my life, and returned to them often.

And now I was discovering that in the withering furnace of affliction, my leaf was not withering. But those precious streams of living water kept rising up into my heart, refreshing me daily, hourly, moment by moment.

Through the centuries God's suffering people have turned often to the Book of Job. And for me, Job came alive in a new way— as did the prophets Jeremiah, Isaiah, and Daniel, whose suffering foreshadowed the agony of Christ. They became my companions as I walked through the valley.

For the first time I could understand and truly appreciate the tortured cry of Jesus in the Garden of Gethsemane: "Father, if thou be willing, remove this cup from me" (Luke

22:42). God's Word kept me from unwarranted guilt and negative thinking, leading me out of a maze of depression; and always with the assurance that, in spite of everything, God was still in control. He was upholding the universe and me.

As I look at many young people in our society today, one message keeps coming to me: here are lives out of control. They don't want to be controlled because control requires responsibility. So they have adopted life-styles and attitudes of irresponsibility.

They communicate a philosophy that says the world is out of control, and here is where the Christian can give unwavering testimony. Once we are in God's kingdom, we acknowledge that he is King, and he controls even when something happens that seems impossible to bear. For me, the Word brought acceptance, comfort, poise, and a certainty that in spite of everything, "he guards the lives of his faithful ones" (Ps. 97:10, NIV).

As medical bills mounted, the church was eager to help us bear the financial burden. We became objects of a special outpouring of sympathy and love. Gifts appeared regularly in the mail. Nearly every week someone had a scheme for raising money for Danny. There were bake sales, flower sales, car washes. God began to show us something very important and beautiful about the body of Christ: Whenever God's people meet together in any communion they bring with them all their humanity, weaknesses, and yes, their sins.

Some in the church had come from different denominational backgrounds. We didn't see eye-to-eye on everything. An "old guard" had viewed with suspicion some of the "innovations" Henry had instituted. Differences of opinion had left a legacy of small hurts and misunderstandings. But now, with the shadow of death on our home, those petty problems seemed unworthy of mention as differences faded and then disappeared. Through the alchemy of suffering, our hearts were fused into that sweet unity which the songwriter must have had in mind when he wrote, "the fellowship of kindred minds is like to that above."

But beyond the bond that suffering creates between God's people, I felt a new kind of bond, a oneness with all humanity, because *all* humanity suffers. I began to realize that no one you look at, ever, hasn't in some way been touched by pain and sorrow. It was not that I had been singled out by God for some special ordeal. All over the world, people live in various stages of suffering. People are in the process of losing loved ones. There are thousands of others who have lost two-year-old children.

When we would take Danny to the Ann Arbor hospital for treatment, we would line up with seventy or eighty other families. There it dawned on me that I was not all that unique. I, too, was part of the fabric of humanity's dark side, its sin, its curse, its suffering and death. Suffering was giving me a new perspective on life, and at the same time it was convincing me more than ever that the greatest need of man is to know the One who said, "I am the resurrection, and the life: he that believeth in me, though he were dead, yet shall he live" (John 11:25).

While I was going through *my* Gethsemane, Henry was going through his, but at times it seemed as though we were traveling different roads. Often suffering creates special ties between husband and wife, and I am sure that Danny's did for us, and yet not in the way one might suppose. Henry had grown up without a mother, estranged from his father, and he found it difficult to bare his heart to anyone, even to his wife.

In the darkest moments of his life, he sometimes seemed imprisoned in a shell of silence. We usually went to the Word, prayed, and agonized separately. Often the first inkling I had of what was going through Henry's mind would be when I would type his sermon notes. The inner turmoil, which he found so difficult to share with any individual, he somehow found the freedom to speak of when he stood in the pulpit.

I particularly remember one Sunday morning when Henry revealed that during the long nights he had tearfully demanded of God, "Why, why have you taken this son for whom we have such plans? This son whom we consecrated to you?" Then Henry went on to speak of God's answer to the question: "Is it not enough that I understand and have given my own Son over to such pain? Is it not enough that I care about your grief?"

That night a reply was wrung from Henry's tormented heart. "It is enough, Lord."

In February, six months after the first signs of the disease, Danny suffered a brain hemorrhage. Now he could no longer speak clearly. Though his mind was still alert, his muscles would not respond as he strained to formulate familiar sounds that would express his need. The eyes, so large and blue against his pale, thin face, pleaded for understanding.

Then one morning, soon after, we were startled to note the absence of the familiar sounds with which Danny usually greeted us. Quickly we made our way into the dining room. We stood speechless. Danny was no longer there. Only the pale, wasted shell of what had been his earthly house, remained. Our son was at last at peace.

The little town of Sherwood fell unusually quiet as word of Danny's death spread from post office to gas station to telephone party line. While the town mourned with us, we, for the first time, undertook the melancholy chores encompassed by the term "funeral arrangements"—the selection of a burial plot, a headstone, and a small casket. The satin-lined box, had it a happier function, would have been described as cute, but as the final resting place of a two-year-old child, its tiny dimensions seemed a cruel reminder of the power of death.

On March 23, a cold, blustery day, we gathered at the church for Danny's funeral. We who had so often mourned with others were this day mourners ourselves. It was a strange sensation, unreal, as though we were going through motions in a trance, or being manipulated like puppets. Was this really happening to us?

After the little box was lowered into the spaded earth, church people and friends climbed into their cars and faded off into the landscape. We stood almost alone with our son, Leon. The wind was blowing hard now, whipping a cold drizzle into our faces. Standing beside us was our music director, Byron Hosmer.

"What would you like to do tonight?" Byron asked softly.

"How can we best think about heaven?" Henry responded in a strong voice.

"I know," Byron said, "why don't we take in an orchestra concert at Battle Creek?"

So we drove to the concert hall that night and listened to the violins and trumpets. They reminded us of God's great orchestra, that one day we would be hearing heavenly music, and that Danny was already there.

THREE

A Second Countdown to Tragedy

On campus, Henry was the kind of person that was not easily ignored. He was a senior, loud, cocky, a varsity baseball player. He seemed bent on proving that he was a man, tough, in control. But whatever his faults, it was generally agreed that Henry Steel was fun, a guy everyone liked.

Above all, Henry loved his Lord unashamedly. He had declared himself a ministerial student, and those who had heard him preach affirmed that he possessed unusual power and eloquence for so young a man. Already he was in constant demand to supply pulpits in the area. *Someday*, I told myself, *I would like to date Henry Steel*.

The following year, Henry had intended to enroll in Spring Arbor Junior College, though he was unable to do so. Without assistance from home he could not pay his tuition and had been forced to drop out for a year to work. He found a job in an automobile plant in Flint.

To help with expenses, he had his sights on a partial scholarship offered by the denomination to the youth soliciting the largest number of subscriptions to the church youth magazine. In the competition, Henry's closest competitor was a determined young lady from Temperance—me. With our church's energetic new pastor, Larry Burr, urging me on, I felt certain I would land the prize.

The following fall, my senior year in high school, I was standing in the registration line, scanning the scores of new and unfamiliar faces when I saw Henry. Feeling inexplicably excited, I summoned all my courage and called his name. "Henry, Henry Steel." He whirled around, and his eyes met mine. I had learned that Henry was my closest rival in the magazine contest but I had not yet heard the results. "Who won the scholarship?" I asked. "Do you know?"

"Valetta," he said softly, seeming somehow different from the brash senior who had graduated the year before, "if it weren't for that scholarship I would still be working at Fisher Body. The Lord did so many great things to supply my financial needs. I know he wants me here in college." Then he added gently, "I'm sorry, though, that you lost."

"I'm really glad you won it, Henry," I replied, with a sincerity that surprised me. "I really am."

Back in the dorm I finished unpacking, excitedly reporting the events of the summer to my roommate, Margaret. Then I headed for the dining hall. At the front steps I noticed Henry.

"Hi." I smiled. "How are things going?"

"Oh, fine," he replied.

Then he shattered our small talk with a question. "Valetta, how about getting together tonight for the opening reception?"

Henry Steel asking me for a date? I struggled to conceal my excitement, paused a moment as though pondering the question, and then in a voice that I desperately hoped sounded calm and mature beyond my sixteen years replied, "Sure, that would be great. What time should we meet?"

I could hardly wait to get back to my room. "Margaret," I gasped, "you won't believe what just happened! Henry Steel is back, and he just asked me for a date tonight. I am so excited! I think he is the neatest guy on campus."

The reception that evening took place on

the broad stretch of lawn in back of the administration building. As we walked toward the refreshment table, the breeze felt suddenly cool on my skin. Instinctively, I clasped my arms around me for warmth. Henry paused in the middle of a story about his work at Fisher Body, took off his big sweater, and draped it around my shoulders. Engulfed in his blue cardigan, my face turned red.

"It was so stupid of me to forget a sweater," I stammered.

"What?" Henry responded in mock offense. "You mean you don't like my sweater?"

Soon it was curfew time for high school students. "Well, this will be the end," I told myself. Henry, by asking me out, had made one gallant gesture to his rival in the scholarship contest. The magic spell was about to break. Tomorrow classes would begin, and then it would be back to reality.

"Good night, Henry," I said.

"One question before 'good night,'" he replied. "How about having dinner with me Friday night?"

"OK, well, sure, I would be glad to," I stammered again, trying not to show the surge of pleasure I felt.

As I climbed up the steps to my room and looked over my schedule, I realized with some regret that I had not left much time for dating. I was carrying a load of five subjects, singing in a mixed quartet, working part time for the school registrar, and practicing basketball two nights a week. My unscheduled time that remained would have to be devoted to study, and plenty of it, if I wanted to keep up my grade point average.

Several weeks later, after turning down Henry's invitation to "get together" for the third night in a row, explaining that I had to study, Henry looked at me disapprovingly. "Why do you have to be such a slave to your studies?" he argued. "What's the point? School is not the real world, you know. Once you walk out the door, you'll discover what life is all about, and that's when what you have really learned will count, not whether you got straight A's."

Unless I studied hard I could never preserve my straight-A record. The thought of letting my grades slip frightened me. My academic record spelled a kind of security to me—a security I very much needed. "Learning is an important process," I answered. "Besides, it helps one develop discipline." I had to admit, though, that in more than one class my only motive to study was the pursuit of another A.

Not easily discouraged, Henry had other

schemes that would offer opportunity for us to see each other. He suggested my quartet accompany him Sunday evenings to a little church where he sometimes preached. When I played basketball, Henry would organize an impromptu pep squad consisting of his buddies to provide vociferous encouragement. With the sound of his voice rising in unrestrained enthusiasm above the others, my face would turn red to the delight of my teammates. One Friday that fall, as our quartet left for a long weekend of meetings, Larry, a tall senior in our group turned to me, and with a sly twinkle in his eye said, "You know, Valetta, Henry has another girl back home."

The next day after dinner Henry suggested that we go for a walk. The October sun felt warm and the leaves were turning. We strolled past a few quiet houses to a small field. Henry paused and looked at the ground. "There is something I feel I need to tell you," he began slowly. "You see, there is this girl back home in my church in Flint, and now, well, I'm starting to care about you. I am asking God to show me his will. So I have decided to go home this weekend. I just wanted you to know that."

Since Larry had told me about the "other girl," I too had been praying that if Henry's friendship was in God's plan, that he would show me. "Henry, all that I want is God's perfect will for our lives," I said. "Let's pray that God will guide you in whatever decision you make as you go home." We bowed our heads and prayed. I then pondered Psalm 138:8: "The Lord will work out his plans for my life—for your lovingkindness, Lord, continues forever" (TLB).

The following week we walked past a few quiet houses to a vacant lot. The wind sent shivers through me, and I stepped up the pace. Henry reached for my arm. "Let's stop," he said, and then looking intently into my eyes he began to speak softly. "I believe I care for you a lot," he said, "so I have broken up with the girl back home. Could we become steady friends like regular dates and all?"

I paused, suddenly aware of my heart thumping wildly, and I struggled to form a suitable response. All that came out was a simple, "Yes, Henry, of course." Somehow I could not yet tell him how much I cared.

Then he took my hands in his and drew me towards him. "May I kiss you?" he asked.

Two years later, on a sweltering July day, we were married in my home church in Temperance. It was a simple ceremony, but the little church was packed. By this time I had completed my freshman year of college, just one year behind Henry. Our financial resources were all but depleted.

We moved into a small trailer on the outskirts of Lambertville, determined to work a year, save our money, and continue our schooling at Roberts Wesleyan College at North Chili, New York. I found a secretarial job working for the DeVilbiss Company, and Henry worked at Willy's Overland, helped Dad with building projects, and served as our church's youth pastor.

Our minister at this time, Larry Burr, was to prove a key influence in Henry's development. Energetic and creative, Larry had broken out of the mold of provincial denominationalism and caught a vision for the world. Missions to him was not merely a project of the Ladies' Auxiliary, represented by somber, drably garbed spinsters presiding over a table of native dolls and Oriental curiosities. No, missions was the greatest task in the world, the enterprise nearest the heart of God, something to get excited about and to give one's life for. How his vision would become Henry's vision, and one day so alter the course of our lives, I could never have at that time imagined.

Our Sherwood pastorate followed. And after Danny's death and the completion of our third year at Sherwood, Henry and I both sensed the nudge of the Holy Spirit.

Certainly, this was the time for Henry to finish his college education.

We spent that summer, following our resignation, in Temperance, where Henry worked for my father in his lumber business. It was a delightful hiatus between the hectic routine of the parsonage and what we thought would be the beginning of a new school year. There were leisurely hours with the family, time for recreation and rest. Oh, how we needed rest!

Then one afternoon a delegation of laymen from a church in Kalamazoo pulled up in front of Dad's business. Henry had held a series of evangelistic meetings in the church a short time earlier and recognized the spokesman of the committee, a man named Wilson Hibbard. After some pleasantries, Wilson disclosed the purpose of their visit.

"Henry, our pastor is about to retire, and we are looking for a replacement," he began. "We've prayed about it, and we are convinced that you are the man."

"Gentlemen," Henry replied, "I'm honored by your request, but we have already enrolled in a college. In fact, our furniture has been moved to an apartment there."

After the men left, I saw Henry standing strangely quiet with his head down. Slowly he turned to me. "I answered them before even praying," he said. Then with a sigh, he added, "Valetta, I have a strange impression that God wants me in Kalamazoo. I feel uneasy about going back to school. Somehow I sense the time is short, as though for some reason it is important that I get back into the work."

We agreed to put out a kind of fleece. "Lord," Henry said, "if this impression, which humanly speaking does not make sense, is really of you, lead the committee from the Kalamazoo church to approach me again."

Two weeks later, a long-distance call came from Wilson Hibbard. "Henry," he began, "I'm calling to see if you will reconsider your decision." For Henry that meant school would have to wait.

In September we moved to Kalamazoo. Living with us now were my sister Leonora (Lea), in nurse's training, and our youth minister, Frank Gorsline, who had found Christ through Henry's ministry in Sherwood. Kalamazoo, peopled largely by stolid families of Dutch descent, was inviting, clean, and distinguished for its economic prosperity and low rate of unemployment. It had been dubbed the average American city, and a scale model of the town had been displayed at the 1958 World's Fair in Brussels, Belgium. The area's paper mill had also earned an appellation, "the paper city." Intellectual and religious influences stemmed from the town's numerous colleges and churches.

We had been in Kalamazoo only three weeks when our daughter, Lorna, was born. She put in her appearance on a Sunday morning, a memorable fact in that her arrival wreaked havoc with the usual schedule of services. A blonde little bundle of life, she was as fair as Leon, our second son, was dark. She was endowed with a sunny disposition, a fiery temperament, and an indomitable will. Now between Leon's two-year-old antics, the demands of the nursery responsibilities for our enlarged family, and the constant parade of guests which Henry regularly diverted through the parsonage, our house once more became "Grand Central Station."

In many ways, Kalamazoo was a repetition of our Sherwood experience, only on a larger scale. Every Sunday, Henry's increasingly dynamic preaching attracted new listeners, including students from the nearby colleges. Earlier the church had purchased a site for a new building, and now when Henry proposed a new structure to replace the outmoded and overflowing sanctuary, there was no denying him. The congregation, catching his enthusiasm, rallied to the cause. A building committee was formed.

The old property was sold to the Upjohn Company, and ground was broken for the new sanctuary. Henry, clear to all, was a man marked for success.

Life was settling again into a comfortable routine. It had never been so promising for us. But again the shadow began to approach. First, it hardly seemed to be a shadow at all, but gradually it began to extend like a long, dark hand, reaching around the circumference of our lives.

The following fall, after we had been in Kalamazoo one year, Henry was troubled by a persistent cough—a mere chest cold, he told himself. At the same time, while driving, he found it difficult to turn the steering wheel with his left arm. A few mornings later as he shaved, he was puzzled because one side of his neck appeared considerably larger than the other. I insisted he see a doctor.

After a cursory exam, the doctor concluded that the problem was a glandular infection. When antibiotics produced no effect, however, the doctor decided to do a biopsy. Though the report was negative, Henry felt strangely apprehensive.

During the winter months the swelling increased. Lea, now a registered nurse, urged Henry to see a specialist. A month later Henry visited Dr. Liddig, who after examining Henry's neck scheduled him for tests at the nearby Bronson Methodist Hospital. I was told to meet him there.

Stepping outside into the heavenly, gentle snow, I walked up the hill three blocks to the hospital, past the reception desk, onto the elevator, through the nurses station, to Henry's room. Carefully opening the door, I looked in. There sat Henry, on a chair in a white sheet-like hospital gown. He looked so different without his usual suit and tie, and I said, "You sure look funny in that outfit."

"Valetta, I want you to sit down," he said. "I need to talk to you, and I couldn't wait. I think I'll be out of here soon. Actually, they got the reports back, and I told the doctor to level with me. I wasn't prepared, however, for the results."

I sensed a numbness rising somewhere from the pit of my stomach, that same numbness I had felt listening to Danny's diagnosis. "Valetta," Henry continued, "that little lump on my neck is Hodgkin's disease."

"Hodgkin's?" I echoed. "What's that?"

Henry drew a deep breath. "A type of cancer—cancer of the lymph glands. There may be remissions for a time, but it is fatal. Don't be alarmed, honey, because there is a lot of hope, and God is on our side."

"But," I stammered, "you've never been sick. You can't possibly be sick, not with cancer. You are only twenty-six!"

"We do have time," Henry went on. "We can go on a year, maybe two: we must spend it wisely. Somehow I feel it should be invested for something that will outlast my own life, and I want to talk to you about that."

Prior to that conversation, two events had combined to rivet Henry's attention on foreign missions. First were the dramatic deaths of five young missionaries, martyred for Christ in an attempt to reach a remote tribe of Ecuadorian headhunters, the Aucas, with the gospel. The second was the coming of Henry's mentor, and my Temperance pastor, Larry Burr, to our area for a missionary rally.

Larry had felt led to leave the pastorate and join a missionary organization, the Oriental Missionary Society (now OMS International). With Larry's coming, Henry began to sense the relevance of foreign missions to the local church. As the two men sat talking late one night, Henry expressed his desire to be personally involved in making Christ known beyond the borders of his homeland. Finally he put the question to Larry: "Do you think God might have a place for me in missions?"

"Henry," Larry responded thoughtfully, "if God has put that kind of a desire in your heart, there is no doubt that he is right now preparing you for a future in missionary work. Perhaps, when your work is finished here in Kalamazoo, he will lead you to OMS."

That Sunday night, as Henry had sat on his hospital bed pondering his clouded future, he suddenly felt that he and Larry must talk. Larry had been holding a rally at Vicksburg, a small town a few miles from Kalamazoo. Henry reached him there and said, "Larry, how would you like to preach my funeral sermon?" Larry had known Henry long enough to take this kind of banter without flinching. "Why sure, Henry, any time. You name the place and time, and I'll be there."

"No, Larry, this time I'm serious. I'm in the hospital right now, and the doctors have diagnosed my problem as Hodgkin's disease, cancer of the lymph glands."

There was a long silence. "Look, Henry, I will be right over to see you after this service."

That evening the two men who had already shared so much together talked in subdued voices, as men do when awed with a view of life in an entirely new perspective. "The doctors say I may have no more than a year or two to live, and perhaps as little as six months," Henry said. "How do you think I should spend them?"

"Well, Henry," Larry proposed, "if you have the strength, I think you should take a trip to some mission field, preach to those who have never heard, and you will rejoice to see those faces in eternity."

"Pray with me about it, Larry," Henry said. "This may be just what God wants me to do."

With Henry back home, looking and sounding little different from the Henry I had always known, my mind was numb. But now the whole sequence of events had an awful familiarity. We had been through the "countdown" with Danny, and here it was on us again. Somehow the heart cannot accept what the mind insists is true. I found myself struggling to awaken from a bad dream.

The following Sunday, Henry stood before the congregation. His voice sounded strong and even. Calmly, he announced the results of the hospital tests, concluding, "We can only go ahead and do the work God has given us to do. This is all any of us can do."

The doctors had arranged for Henry to undergo a series of treatments which hopefully would retard the progress of the disease. The first of these was controlled exposure to X rays.

When we arrived at the hospital, a group of doctors were waiting. They talked in cold, professional tones and in that mysterious, somehow frightening, medical jargon. Henry was clad in an embarrassingly short hospital gown. He felt uncomfortably conspicuous. He sensed that in their eyes he was just another case history, a diseased organism, an individual without identity. "I have never felt so alone in my whole life," he confided to me.

Carefully the doctors arranged him on the table, under the frighteningly imposing eye of the huge machine. Steel doors closed about him. From his prone position he could see the doctors looking down on him through the narrow glass of the observation window. There followed an eerie silence, broken suddenly by a deep hum that rose from the heart of the machine, louder and louder. He knew his body was being bombarded by invisible forces that had power to inhibit the growth of the malevolent cells within his body.

The side effects to the treatment were immediate and violent. Though permitted to go home, Henry was frequently seized with a violent nausea which left him so weak he could hardly climb the stairs to his bedroom. He would ascend a few steps at a time. He was steadily losing weight and was almost never free from a debilitating cough.

Now again, as it happened during the long vigil with Danny, day by day God opened to me the sweet resources of his Word in special ways. Through the Word, the Holy Spirit can work a curious alchemy which transmutes pain into comfort, and crushing sorrow into sweetness. Romans 8:28, a verse so time-worn it has almost become a cliché, was expounded anew to my heart by the Comforter. God would bring good out of this. How? I could not fathom, but he would. I would keep watching for that good. Yes, I would look for miracles, and it would be an adventure.

F O U R

Borne Up along the Way of the Cross

But, now, what next? The doctors' prognosis, six months, perhaps a year, drastically altered our perspective on the future career of Rev. and Mrs. Henry Steel. As we turned to the Word for guidance, God gave us 1 Peter 4:19: "So if you are suffering according to God's will, keep on doing what is right and trust yourself to God who made you, for he will never fail you" (TLB).

For the present, at least, we believed that God would have us carry on in what we were doing. We determined to take each day as it came, to live in "day-tight compartments," giving ourselves to the things that mattered. It had never been so easy to sort through the mundane affairs of life and focus on the "important." As Ben Jonson once said, "The prospect of immediate death wonderfully concentrates the mind."

"Maybe God wants to heal Henry for his glory," many suggested. We believed in healing, had seen God heal others. Now, certainly, if anyone had the right to ask for divine healing as his children, we too had that right. A group of ministers came and prayed for Henry, anointing him with oil as instructed in Scripture (James 5:14). After they prayed, Henry began responding to treatments and strength returned.

"Do you feel that God has touched you?" Dale Cryderman asked Henry one day.

"I don't doubt that God has touched me," Henry responded, "but I don't feel that I can say it will be permanent. The doctors say the disease is in remission. Whatever God has for me, though, I pray I'll accept it. My desire is that God will do with my life whatever will bring him the most glory."

Listening to Henry's response, it dawned on me that some deep change was taking place in my husband. There was a quiet poise; yes, a nobility in his sincere, unaffected response that was foreign to the old Henry I had known. God was doing something beautiful in this man, a kind of work of art. Yes, I remembered, "all things work together for good" (Rom. 8:28).

Sensing we needed to get away and be

alone to reflect, our people suggested that we take a short vacation to Florida at their expense. Those were blissful days in that picture-postcard setting. We were sweethearts as never before, hand in hand, splashing together in the surf, each experience so sweet, so painfully sweet.

Watching Henry stand tall against the waves and wind, I felt my heart throb with excruciating affection for this courageous man. A cry arose unbidden from my heart, "Oh, Lord, you know how much I love him, how much I need him." Psalm 90:12 became a kind of theme verse for us at that time. "Teach us to number our days and recognize how few they are; help us to spend them as we should" (TLB).

Back in Kalamazoo, Henry continued to fulfill his responsibilities as pastor, but now, every Sunday, it seemed that he preached with increasing intensity. One morning, looking into the face of the congregation, he spoke fervently, "When we know there are very few tomorrows left, we face some very embarrassing questions. Have I spent too much time finding little answers to little questions? Have I spoken out for Christ only when it was easy to speak for him, repeating the gospel to those who have heard it hundreds of times while millions have never heard it once? Someday, we tell ourselves, with a little more preparation, experience, and opportunity, then. . . . But suddenly we realize there will be no more time for preparation, no more experience, no better opportunity. Geographic boundaries and denominational lines vanish, and we see a lost world. No man should live his life presuming on 'tomorrow.' In eternity there are millions of people who would give everything they have had in this world in order to come back into it for one more day—to do the one thing they had been putting off—right up to the day that they died. No doubt the greatest thing that ever happened to me was to be told by a physician, 'No man can tell you how long it will be.'"

As I listened to Henry's words, I knew he was about to make an announcement that would shake the congregation. For some time he had been in contact with OMS International, the missionary organization which Larry Burr now served. While attending the OMS annual convention at Winona Lake, Indiana, Henry had shared with their vice-president, Bill Gillam, a growing conviction that God was urging him to invest the remaining months of his life in the cause of missions.

When the OMS board met the next week,

they did something unprecedented. In view of Henry's unique call and special gifts, they voted to waive the usual health requirements and invited him to join the society. The plan was that he should take a preliminary trip to South America to better acquaint himself with the work of the mission, and then head the regional office in Portland, Oregon.

When the congregation learned of Henry's decision, there was mixed response. For some there were tears. People expressed their surprise; some voiced disagreement and questioned the practicality of our choice. After all, was it really wise for a dying man, with perhaps no more than months to live, to leave a secure pastorate and the bosom of a loving congregation?

The next week a group of key laymen invited Henry to lunch in one of the city's finest restaurants. After a sumptuous meal, a spokesman turned to Henry. "Look at it this way, Pastor," he began, "we want you; we need you. We believe that God still has work for you in Kalamazoo. If your life is cut short by illness, Valetta and the kids will need security, and we can give that to them here." There was a calculated pause while the man waited for his words to register. Then he went on. "We're prepared to make you an offer. If you remain here in Kalamazoo, we will guarantee that your children will be provided for through college. What do you say?"

Later, in addressing a group of missionaries about what it means to cast oneself in faith on God, Henry recalled that moment. "Don't think that it didn't come as a tremendous temptation," he said. "The devil told me I was a fool to turn down an offer like that. But as I looked into the faces of those generous men with their promises of security, an answer came to me. It wasn't my answer but God's. There is no security, I told them, outside the will of God."

The Hodgkin's disease continued in a state of remission for a full year, far longer than we had dared hope. We saw the new church completed. And now, with each succeeding day of apparently normal life, came a wistful anticipation that possibly the cancer was no longer there. God had heard our cries, we hoped. A miracle had occurred. Henry had been healed. In a short time we would complete another year at the Kalamazoo church, and Henry would leave on his South American trip, the beginning of service with OMS.

A few days before his departure for South America, however, came the cruel reminder that Henry was still a dying man. Lying on the bed, mentally reviewing the details of the trip, Henry casually threw his arm across his chest, causing his hand to fall on the back of his neck. What he felt sent a shrill alarm through him. The evil lumps had emerged again. His fingers burned as though the malignant cells were made of fire. For a moment his spirit faltered.

New X-ray treatments were hastily administered. Henry, armed with a supply of pills, went ahead with the planned tour; but from that time on, indications of the disease appeared with increasing frequency. Painful treatments preceded extensive periods of weakness and gradual recuperation. The short intervals between these treatments marked the relentless march of the malignancy in Henry's body, and served as a cruel chronometer reminding us of his dwindling life expectancy.

Henry's South American tour and our subsequent move to Portland proceeded in spite of our bouts with the disease. Though increasingly frail in health, Henry kept a pace that would have staggered a healthy man. In addition to arranging the itineraries of scores of missionaries, he himself was in constant demand as a missionary speaker and evangelist at churches and camps throughout the Northwest.

Although Henry avoided mention of his

physical condition, his increasing discomfort finally forced him to visit a Christian specialist in Portland who took a personal interest in Henry. Dr. Williams diagnosed his most recent problems as spastic colitis. He was convinced that Henry's system could no longer accept the severe X-ray bombardments, and Henry was forced to begin the alternative and even more excruciating nitrogen mustard gas treatments. Each dose left the patient so violently sick that for a while he cared little whether he lived or died. To a visiting friend Henry once confided, "I dread the gas. I dread it with a passion."

With the progression of the disease, and a bout with pneumonia, came increasing lung congestion. From this time on, he seldom enjoyed a good night's sleep, and he spoke with a continual wheeze. Every word was an effort. To find relief from the lung congestion, he would often throw himself face down across the bed while dictating letters into the dictaphone on the floor, and yet there was no thought of stopping.

With the increasingly brief periods of remission, following the painful mustard gas treatments, Henry would be on the road again. His now well-known message, *A Dying Man Speaks to Dying Men*, held congregations transfixed and produced profound results. Recalling revival services which Henry held at this time—services in which an entire Mormon family once came to Christ—a pastor remarked, "Those services were the most fruitful our church has ever had since its organization."

Each week as Henry would come home, and I washed his shirts, ironed them, and packed them again, I would wrestle with a tumult of conflicting feelings. While I was deeply grateful for the joy and exhilaration he derived from expending every last ounce of mortal breath and energy for the sake of his Master, I missed each moment he was away. I needed him, and his children needed him. The precious remaining sands of time were pouring so quickly through the hourglass of his life. So little time remained.

Bob Bletcher, our local pastor, invited Henry for a week of combined missionary-evangelistic services. I was grateful the meetings were near home where Leon, Lorna, and I could attend. As I sat there nightly, I detected a new quality in Henry's preaching. He spoke with almost a total lack of self-consciousness. He seemed to see himself as an embodied illustration of the gospel—which proclaims life through death. Somehow, I believe that in his lonely hours, as he walked the way of the Cross with Christ, he died to Henry Steel. He identified with Christ in a new way, and he loved to quote Philippians 1:20-21: "So that now as always Christ will be exalted in my body, whether by life or by death. For to me, to live is Christ and to die is gain" (NIV).

As he spoke, he would dramatize the sensation of sitting across from the doctor and being told he was a dying man. "But don't feel sorry for me because the doctors say I do not have long to live," he would go on. "There is no difference, really, between you and me, except for maybe a few years. None of us really knows. For all of us, when we stand before Christ, it will not be a matter of how old we are or of what age we died, but of what we did with Jesus Christ."

One night I glanced over at Leon as Henry spoke. He sat in the pew beside me as though frozen. His eyes were fixed on his father with remarkable intensity for a seven-year-old. That night, shortly after we had gone to bed, I heard Leon crying. I hurried into his room. "Mommy," he sobbed, "I just saw Jesus dying on the cross in my dreams."

A few weeks later, I took the children with me to Seattle for the closing night of one of Henry's conferences. That evening he spoke on knowing Christ. After the service, I was starting to leave the sanctuary with the pastor's wife when I heard a small voice. It was Leon's. "Mom," he said, "can I stay with Dad?"

Sometime later that evening Henry and Leon walked into the parsonage, smiling. "Valetta," Henry said as we got ready for bed, "this was a very special night for me. Something exciting happened. Leon asked me if he was old enough to become a Christian. You know, I asked the Lord if he would let me lead my son to him before I went to heaven, and tonight he gave me that joy."

When the OMS board convened in Winona Lake in 1962, it made a decision that left me temporarily unhappy and shaken. Impressed with the outstanding work Henry had done in the Northwest, the board asked him to move to mission headquarters in Los Angeles to take charge of all homeland ministries.

"But Henry," I pleaded, "I don't want to move. I'm perfectly happy where we are, and what about your doctor? Who can possibly replace Dr. Williams?"

"Valetta, you may not understand this," Henry soothed, "but I believe God wants me to walk through every open door. I know it doesn't make sense, since there are so many uncertainties about the future, but somehow I'm sure that this is the next step he wants us to take."

In Los Angeles, the famed City of Hope Hospital, outstanding as a cancer research center, admitted Henry as a patient. Henry would check into the City of Hope for the painful treatments required to prolong his dwindling life span. "Well, Valetta," Henry said one day, trying to effect a jaunty joviality I'm sure he didn't feel, "I guess we'll just have to move my office here to the hospital. They want me to check in and stay a little longer this time."

That is what we did. Now, instead of brainstorming in the office, I sat beside his hospital bed while he shared his restless passion to awaken the churches of America to a vision of a world dying without Christ. To the doctors and nurses who knew Henry's condition all too well, but could hardly fathom the burning impulses that drove him on, it must have seemed an aberration of the mind.

Here was a man, as it were, standing on the verge of the grave, yet making plans and dreaming dreams, devising schemes for a future that he would never see. It was irrational, a kind of a madness. One afternoon while Henry dozed, I strolled up and down the hospital corridors, passing ward after ward of patients, all terminally ill, and Henry was among them. Yes, here was my husband. He too was numbered among the living dead. I began to weep. Tears kept flowing.

As Henry's lungs deteriorated, clogged with growths and scarred by cobalt, each breath became an effort. Nauseated, he found it difficult to keep anything down, and he was put on a special diet. His heart was showing signs of irregularities, side effects of the chemotherapy.

"Lord," I cried one day, "Henry is not getting better, he is getting worse, much worse." At the same time I could not relinquish hope. After the treatment and nausea would come remission, blessed remission, and with it time, that most precious of all commodities. Once more Henry responded to treatments: the growths in the lungs began to shrink, and before long he was back home.

Those priceless days, like the last and best perfume in a bottle, Henry determined to pour out upon his Savior. A week after his return home from the hospital, he flew to the OMS Atlanta office to work with Paul and Vi Haines, then on to Indiana where he was keynote speaker at a convention. Following this came consultation with Howard and Wilma Jacob who headed the OMS office at Winona Lake.

"How long do you think Henry will be able to keep up the roadwork?" a missionary colleague asked me. I thought of Christ's words, "Take therefore no thought for the morrow: for the morrow shall take thought for the things of itself. Sufficient unto the day is the evil thereof" (Matt. 6:34).

"Well," I said, "the Lord doesn't ask us to try to solve tomorrow's problems today." Then I added, "I think Henry will travel just as long as he can." Little did I realize that in the weeks just ahead there would be more traveling for Henry and me than we had ever imagined possible. One long final journey would take him to the very portals of his heavenly home.

A few weeks later, just before Thanksgiving, I received a phone call from Henry. He was still in Indiana. I could sense the excitement in his voice. "Valetta," he said, "how would you like to take a trip with me around the world?"

"You're kidding."

"No, really, someone is writing a blank check for us to take a trip, both of us. They are suggesting we go to Europe, to the Holy

Land, wherever we wish. I feel maybe God wants us to visit the OMS fields in Asia and Greece."

"But, Henry," I sputtered, "what about the children, and who will run things at the office?"

"I know," he answered, "and of course you are wondering about my health. Frankly, so am I. Valetta, why don't you make a list of all the obstacles, and let's pray about each one specifically."

"Henry, you know I'd be thrilled to go if, if. . . ."

"Valetta," he put in, "let's just trust God for some miracles."

Les Ike, our mission treasurer, and his wife, Pat, offered to take care of Leon in our absence, and our dear friend, Flo Rickards, who worked in our Men for Missions office, insisted that she stay with Lorna. One more hurdle remained. Henry knew he dare not make a trip without the approval of his doctors at the City of Hope.

"You're a very sick man," the doctors agreed, "but if problems develop, you can always fly home. We see no real danger in your going."

OMS leaders agreed reluctantly. "We feel hesitant about letting you make such a strenuous trip in your condition," they explained. "It hardly seems wise, and yet if

God is leading you, who are we to say no?"

It seemed that God had removed every obstacle. We called a missions travel agent, Howard Hill, and asked him to write out our tickets. Our itinerary would take us to Greece, India, Japan, Korea, Hong Kong, Taiwan, Hawaii, and back to Los Angeles.

We left New York in a snowstorm, and by the time we reached Athens, the first stopover on our itinerary, it was clear to me that Henry was experiencing increasing discomfort. His persistent cough was worse. He was running a high fever and felt nauseated. When OMS missionaries met us at the airport, we agreed that Henry should be under a doctor's care. A doctor soon admitted him to a Greek hospital.

I was assailed by doubts and on the verge of despair. Had we been out of our minds to think of attempting an around-the-world trip with Henry so desperately sick? Possibly he was dying in this unfamiliar environment; and we were trying to communicate with medical personnel who knew little English. It was an experience that filled me with uneasiness, bordering on feelings of terror. Armed with a Greek-English dictionary, I shopped little markets at night, hunting for snacks that Henry might like.

Two days after chemotherapy, Henry again revived, almost miraculously it seemed. We boarded the plane for the next leg of our journey. In India we were met by OMS Field Director Wesley Duewel, who was soon to be elected mission president.

We visited the city of Benares—holy to Hindus—on the banks of the famous Ganges River. Mingling with masses of staggering humanity, we watched Hindu pilgrims trying to wash away their sins in the polluted waters. We toured ornate Hindu temples and were shocked by scenes of sexual perversion, depicted in shameless detail on the walls.

On a trip to the villages, I came down with a fever. As I dragged myself along, I looked at Henry stooped with pain. Here we were, two invalids, surrounded by a dismal procession of human beings—impoverished, sad, homeless, blind—shuffling along beside us. It seemed as if the whole world were sick.

We visited one of the churches and listened to our Christian brothers singing their *budjins*, the hauntingly beautiful ethnic music of the Indian people. Wesley told us of believers standing heroically for Christ in the face of ostracism and persecution from Hindu relatives and neighbors. Our time in India left us with hearts freshly wounded for a world without Christ. I later established a memorial fund in Henry's name for the building of churches in India. I knew he would have wanted that.

From India we flew to Hong Kong, that crowded crossroads of the Orient; then on to Korea to see OMS's largest work. At the airport, our missionaries Ed and Elmer Kilbourne, along with dozens of Korean believers, greeted us. "We have prayed you around the world on your journey to heaven," they said. "We believe God is going to visit us through you."

Henry's pain was increasing. Besieged with fits of coughing and nausea, he could sleep for only brief periods. Doctors urged that he be admitted to a hospital, but he would not hear of it. Henry was scheduled to preach each evening to the more than 500 pastors that had gathered for the churches' annual conference. This is what he had come to Korea for, and he would do it even if he died in the pulpit. He did it, sometimes gasping and heaving, but he was sustained somehow through the delivery of each sermon. Those who heard the messages, the last that Henry ever preached from a pulpit, will never forget them.

During the long sleepless nights as Henry struggled for breath, I cast myself upon the Lord in prayer and poured over precious passages of Scripture for courage and comfort. One evening God's presence enveloped me with an overwhelming sweetness. The Holy Spirit seemed to direct me to Isaiah 58:8: "Then shall thy light break forth as the morning, and thine health shall spring forth speedily; and thy righteousness shall go before thee; the glory of the Lord shall be thy reward."

"Lord," I asked, "is this word for Henry? Are you going to heal him right here in Korea?" The next night I was drawn to the same chapter. "Lord," I said, "what does this mean? Do you want me to accept a different kind of healing from what I would desire?"

"Soon," the Holy Spirit whispered to me, "soon Henry's healing will be total and eternal."

From Korea we went on to Taiwan where we were met by OMS Field Director Rolland Rice. Missionaries gathered in the Rices' living room while Henry, reclining on the sofa, talked to them. Hunched over now, and in continual pain, he still managed to visit the churches and to take a trip to beautiful Sun Moon Lake. The final leg of our flight took us to Hawaii for a brief stopover, and then on home to Los Angeles.

Sunday and Monday we reserved for Leon and Lorna and a few close friends. These quiet hours together were filled with hugs and kisses and stories about our trip.

The next evening, I packed Henry's bag and prepared for the leisurely drive to the City of Hope where the doctors were expecting him. As we went out the door, Lorna looked at Henry accusingly.

"Daddy, why are you always sick?" she demanded.

"Sweetie," he answered, "Daddy has been sick since you were a baby, but you must thank Jesus that he has let your daddy live long enough so that you will be able to remember him." Leon looked on silently, his big eyes wistful and sad.

The following day, Henry's lungs became so congested that he was placed in an oxygen tent. The next two days he rested almost continually. On the fourth day, doctors told me Henry was on the critical list. I stayed through the night praying there would be yet another remission.

I listened to the oxygen equipment pumping away, and Henry's labored breathing in rhythm with the machine. Like some kind of mechanical octopus, the machine seemed as if it were reaching out and seizing my husband's body. I was losing him. Late in the evening I left the hospital to drive home for a few hours of rest. As I followed the stream of red taillights, I found myself thinking of the funeral. What kind of funeral would Henry want?

I had been home only a few hours when the phone rang. I picked it up. The voice on the other end was cold, impersonal. "I have sad news for you, Mrs. Steel," the doctor began. Just seven days after arriving home from our world trip, Henry had embarked on a new journey to a better place.

He had wanted to be buried in the Sherwood Cemetery in a small plot of ground where we had laid our firstborn, Danny, to rest. The funeral would be held in the new sanctuary of the Kalamazoo church, which stood as a monument to the vision God had given Henry. On May 5, Leon, Lorna, and I, accompanied by OMS President Dr. Eugene Erny, boarded a flight from Los Angeles to Chicago. When our plane touched down at O'Hare International Airport, friends were on hand to meet us and escort us to Kalamazoo.

As the funeral service began, I took my place at the front of the church. Beside me sat Lorna, minus her two front teeth, a normal six year old; and beside her sat Leon, dark and tall for his eight years. My thoughts wandered back over my life with Henry—our first meeting on the campus of the Spring Arbor College, our growing friendship, working together on the yearbook and school paper, the chime of wedding bells, our first pastorate in the quiet little town of Sherwood, the building of this lovely church, and the miracle years in missions. A whole chapter of my life was ending like the final pages of a book.

That afternoon, I felt God take my hand in a way that was almost more literal than figurative. His Spirit reached out to embrace me through a host of loving people: family ministers, missionaries, friends from Sherwood and Kalamazoo. Suddenly, in my mind's eye, I had a vision of my husband, now in his resurrected body, triumphant, no longer burdened with pain, running eagerly to meet his Lord. Jesus, with outstretched arms, was saying to him, "Well done, thou good and faithful servant" (Matt. 25:21). Frank Gorsline, a lad whom Henry had led to Christ years before in Sherwood, now under appointment as a missionary to Brazil, stood to sing a song that so aptly summed up the spirit of Henry Steel:

The path that I have trod,
Has brought me nearer God,
Though often led through sorrow's gate,
Though not the way I choose,
In my way I might lose
The joy that yet for me awaits.

Not what I wish to be,
Nor where I wish to go,

For who am I that I should choose my way.
The Lord shall choose for me,
'Tis better far I know,
So let him bid me go or stay.

After the funeral, Dad approached me. "Valetta," he said, "we have a place for you in our business, and a house is waiting. You know we would love to have you back in Temperance."

"I'll think about it," I responded, but deep within myself I knew my mind was already made up. Henry's call had been my call. God had led us out of the pastorate to invest our lives in missions, and though Henry's task was completed, I did not feel as if I had been released from God's call on my life. The trip to Asia had only deepened my burden for missions and the millions beyond our borders who were without Christ. Moreover, I had found an identity of spirit and an extended family among OMS missionaries. The mission had asked me to continue to work at headquarters. I knew my answer would be yes.

As we left the church that afternoon, Leon had turned to me and solemnly observed, "You know, Mom, this is a great day for Dad, but a sad one for us." I blinked back the tears. His profound words found a painful echo in my heart. Henry's life had been heroic. I could look back over it without a moment's regret. But now the future yawned before me like a vast dark chasm. How could I walk that valley alone? Could I be the kind of parent I ought to be? Without Henry, it all seemed impossible.

FIVE

A Discovery of Identity through Sorrow

I was walking the valley the second time. The first time, when Danny had died, I had had Henry to lean upon. He had been my tower of strength, the one human being I instinctively turned to for comfort and counsel, the one I had clung to when the billows of life threatened to overwhelm me. But now it was different. Henry was gone, out of my earthly life forever. I ached for human arms to hold me in my sorrow, human hands to wipe away my tears.

As the full significance of Henry's death settled down on me, it was at first as though I were caught in a vacuum, or as though all the clocks in the world had suddenly stopped. Time was standing still. I felt engulfed in an interminable aching void.

The day after I returned to Los Angeles from the funeral, I got up as usual, sent the kids off to school, and then walked across the street to the OMS headquarters building where I had my office. I entered through the same doors and passed the same familiar desks and faces, but it was not the same. The landscape of my life had now changed irrevocably.

I sat down to read the mail and glanced over at Henry's empty chair—one of many he would never sit in again. I noticed a stack of letters on his desk—letters he would never answer. Suddenly wave upon wave of grief swept over me. "Lord," I prayed, "I need a miracle just to get through this day."

And always there was the house to go back to. We had not lived there long, but already it had become home. Every room was tenderly haunted with the ghost of Henry. The halls still echoed with recent conversations, laughter, sighs.

I went out to the garage and noticed Henry's books, stacked neatly in boxes against a wall. We had been so busy since coming from Portland, he had not even had time to unpack them. There was his deer rifle, a new Kodak camera, his mounted deer antlers from Montana, hundreds of colored slides from our travels across the U.S.

That was about it, though. Henry didn't

leave many material things, I comforted myself, but he left something infinitely more valuable—an example of a heroic kind of love for his Master. It was a legacy that I would repeatedly draw inspiration from in the months and years ahead.

What should I do with Henry's belongings? His clothing still hung in the closet, his shoes were on the floor, and personal objects were scattered about the room. I decided that for the time being I would leave his things just as they were. Later, when I had come to terms with my grief, I would sort through them, give some of them away, keep others for the children, but not yet.

I was not ready to bear the wrenching act of parting with those memory-laden accoutrements of my husband's mortal life. I have heard that the Jews have a special time for mourning, a time when the bereaved focuses on his grief and weeps. It is a time for release, for cleansing, without guilt, a natural expression of human sorrow. I think this is wise, and I feel God approves. Leon and Lorna saw my tears and shared them. At times I would gather them in my arms, and the three of us would talk of Henry and weep together.

Though I continued working in the same office, I perceived that my role had changed.

For years I had worked as my husband's associate, but now I was passed over in much of the planning and in the brainstorming sessions I so relished.

I felt like a drudge, a misfit. I was routinely pounding out letters on a typewriter. I lived in a man's world, it seemed. *Only men share ideas in this office*, I thought. A woman? What could she contribute? I had ideas, plenty of them, but I had never learned how to sell them. Henry had always done that for me. The administration had listened to him. He was very articulate, and he was a man. *Lord*, I cried inwardly, *help me to find out where I belong*.

For the first time in my life, I was introduced to loneliness. Often in the past, trying to match my husband's frantic pace, I yearned for a patch of solitude. But now I was experiencing a kind of stark loneliness I never really knew existed before. I longed for adult companionship. On weekends, when couples got together for outings or evenings of fellowship, I often was disregarded.

At home, I, who once had prided myself on being in control of things, found it increasingly difficult to cope. One afternoon, Tammy, our big German shepherd, jumped through the screen and began running away. At the same moment Leon and Lorna came in the back door. Their relationship, which, at best, seemed an uneasy truce, had suddenly given way to violence. "Mommy," Lorna screamed, "Leon is hitting me." *Those kids are fighting all the time,* I thought to myself. *How will I ever get them to care for each other?* We had to find the dog. There was dinner to fix, and I didn't feel hungry. "Lord, where can you find good in all of this?" I demanded.

The routines of life called for decisions, always decisions; but I had lost confidence in my ability to make even the simplest decisions. Being decisive required mental energy, and there was no energy to draw from. I was weary. It was an effort just to arrange my jumbled thoughts long enough to solve the most mundane problems. I went through the day's schedule like a robot.

"What, Lord, has happened to my joy, my enthusiasm, my motivation?" I cried out. In the same friendly office, the friendliest face was missing. By contrast, everything seemed cold and lifeless. The little house, where friends used to gather for boisterous, fun-filled evenings, now seemed empty and bare. *If only,* I thought, *Henry could once again walk in that door.* But Henry would never again do that. The thought unleashed waves of depression and self-pity.

The world around me had turned into a featureless plain. People I passed on the streets had no faces; I hardly saw them. Driving over the familiar concrete stretches of the Los Angeles freeway, crowded with automobiles, I felt more isolated than on the country farm where I grew up. On one particular day, absorbed in the tangle of my own thoughts, I missed my turn-offs, suddenly discovering that I did not know where I was, not even sure how to get back home. It seemed somehow symbolic. My life had become like that—a long dull stretch of road that I was traveling, hardly knowing where I was going, or where to get off.

I have shared all of this as frankly as I know how to underscore a plain truth: Christians are in no way exempt from the tragedies of life. We share in the curses and frailities of that nature common to all men. Death, that savage intruder, has the power to break our hearts, to leave us demoralized and, for a time, under the tyranny of despair.

And yet, when the worst that can happen has indeed happened, when the heart is broken, the tears have flowed, and unanswered questions have been wrung in anguish from the soul—a discovery comes. To some it comes sooner, and to some later.

The discovery is simple: God has not left his children without resources.

I had known the comfort of his Word when I cradled my dying son in the little Sherwood parsonage, through the night hours when I tried to quench his unquenchable thirst. Yes, God had spoken then. I had known it in the guest room in Korea as I listened to my husband struggling to draw breath into his tormented lungs; God had spoken both times, and my heart had been at peace. Now he was gently instructing again.

To my surprise and delight, I discovered the Scriptures did indeed bring healing for my latest grief. Every cliché that I had ever heard about his Word was true, really true. It was light in the darkness, bread to the hungry, a staff to the weak, water for parched lips. "The words that I speak unto you," Jesus said, "they are spirit, and they are life" (John 6:63). How true.

I learned, as Amy Carmichael expressed it, to find "gold by moonlight." I started a special notebook in which I stored up my treasures. Many of these verses, long-familiar mottos, were now peculiarly apt, as though the Holy Spirit were fitting them like a skillful tailor to every dimension of my life: "Weeping may endure for a night, but joy cometh in the morning" (Ps. 30:5). "Since the Lord is directing our steps, why try to understand everything that happens along the way?" (Prov. 20:24, TLB). "For it is God who works in you to will and to act according to his good purpose" (Phil. 2:13, NIV). "We can make our plans, but the final outcome is in God's hands" (Prov. 16:1, TLB). "Commit your work to the Lord, then it will succeed" (Prov. 16:3, TLB). "We should make plans—counting on God to direct us" (Prov. 16:9, TLB). "The Lord destroys the possessions of the proud but cares for widows" (Prov. 15:25, TLB).

In the valley of the shadow, like the Psalmist, I had discovered that God's rod and staff—his Word—were indeed my comfort (Ps. 23:4). And like the shepherd's instrument, God used his rod not only for comfort and safety, but also for guidance and correction. God knew there were faulty areas in my life that needed correction. Lovingly, he brought the chastening rod of his Word to bear on those deficiencies.

The first problem which God began to deal with me about was in the area of self-worth. Henry's passing had devastated that part of me. His death left me groping for some kind of identity. Unconsciously I had come to see myself as an adjunct to my dynamic and successful husband. I identified with *his* achievements, realizing my own contributions to them, and basked in the approval that he drew from his colleagues. His ministry gave me opportunities and brought me fulfillment. Now, in a moment, that comfortable role had vanished. I was stripped of my husband and my self-esteem. I was Valetta, alone, no longer Mrs. Steel. Who was I, really? What was I worth?

I looked at myself in the mirror. At thirty I was not very old, but I saw wrinkles. I had experienced a lot of life, and my experience made me cautious. Invitations to go places and try new things that would have been met with enthusiasm ten years earlier, were now greeted with hesitancy and the turmoil of inner questions.

I realized that mentally I was keeping a record book in which I assessed my strengths and weaknesses; it was a kind of ledger. What I was convinced were my true strengths, I listed in the credit column. My weaknesses—areas in which I had experienced feelings of inadequacy and failure—I put in the debit column.

I recalled one disastrous attempt I had made in trying to teach Sunday school. What agony I endured as I tried to ignite a spark of interest while my little students, completely unappreciative of my efforts, proceeded to wiggle and talk. I had come away from that experience with the attitude that I would limit my activities to the safe and comfortable ruts in which I felt secure. I would diligently avoid service opportunities that I perceived to be threatening. I would pride myself on being humble enough to acknowledge my limitations. But was that the way God wanted me to live?

No! And the word he gave me on this subject was John 6:63: "It is the spirit that quickeneth; the flesh profiteth nothing. . . ." It was time, the Holy Spirit seemed to say, to quit mulling over the dreary catalog of my failures; to commit those failures to God, acknowledging that the flesh apart from God is worthless. Even the great successes of the flesh are often negative factors creating rampant pride and rendering us unusable to the Lord. I needed to start trusting the Holy Spirit to bring strength out of my weaknesses.

Coupled with John 6:63, I felt the Holy Spirit urging me on to another verse which I had so glibly quoted in easier times, Philippians 4:13: "I can do all things through Christ which strengtheneth me." My heart really leaped when I grasped that principle. *I am nothing, a big zero, in myself, but Jesus is living in me. His presence in me gives me self-worth. He wants to live out his life in me, enabling me to bring glory to God.*

Other verses that helped underscore this truth, which God was using to change the tenor of my life and the direction of my ministry, were 2 Corinthians 12:9: "I am with you; that is all you need. My power shows up best in weak people" (TLB); and 2 Corinthians 4:7: "But this precious treasure—this light and power that now shine within us—is held in a perishable container, that is, in our weak bodies. Everyone can see that the glorious power within must be from God and is not our own" (TLB).

Still there was another hurdle. I am a woman, and my view of womankind had unconsciously been shaped to a great extent by my culture and family. Almost every daughter's role model is her mother. My mother had passed on to me many strengths: loyalty, responsibility, honesty, and modesty, for instance. However, she had always been one to linger in the background, relinquishing the role of spiritual leader to Dad. With Henry, who was the prototype of the aggressive, self-confident leader, I too had been content to fade into the background. That was woman's place, I had come to accept: behind the scenes, expediently meek and obscure.

Now, as I studied the New Testament, God began to speak to me about my warped view of the woman's role. I believe the gospel has always liberated women. I began to notice that women played a vital part in the spread of early Christianity, for instance. On Paul's missionary journeys, the gospel first took root in the hearts of devoted women. Lydia was the key layperson in the founding of the Philippian church (Acts 16:11-15). Many of Paul's co-workers in missionary enterprises were women. Is it not significant in the Scriptures that contrary to Eastern protocol, Priscilla appears before her husband Aquila (Rom. 16:3)? As a teacher of doctrine, she was possibly more gifted and prominent than her husband. She did not hesitate to exhort and instruct the eloquent evangelist Apollos.

During this time God helped me find acceptance in another problem area—singleness. With Henry gone, I had joined that swelling segment of society which we have designated, or branded, "singles." We lump together in this category those who seem to be life's misfits—individuals who have never been able to land a mate, those whose marriages have come apart, widows and widowers who have been "reduced" to single status by the intervention of premature and untimely death of spouses. The penalty for being single meant exclusion from family-oriented events, a dearth of adult companionship, and long, lonely evenings made even more lonely for want of intimate conversation with a mate.

Were single people really second rate? How did God regard them? Again the Holy Spirit spoke to me through the Word. I read 1 Corinthians 7:17: "But be sure in deciding these matters that you are living as God intended, marrying or not marrying in accordance with God's direction and help, and accepting whatever situation God has put you into" (TLB). And 1 Corinthians 7:7: "But we are not all the same. God gives some the gift of a husband or wife, and others he gives the gift of being able to stay happily unmarried" (TLB).

In my study of the Gospel narratives, I was impressed that Jesus had given of himself to people regardless of their economic or social status. He saw them only as individuals, whether rich, poor, educated, illiterate, married, or single. I determined that I would address people in the same way—as individuals created in God's image. I would recognize what God was doing in their lives. How could I help?

Once I had lost my self-consciousness about being single, I began to feel equally comfortable with families, couples, or other singles. It simply did not matter anymore. I was sure that I was living as Paul had said, "In accordance with God's direction," and for the present that meant being single. There was dignity and honor in that.

Finally, during this period, when God was taking the twisted remnants of my life and reshaping them into a new design, he began to deal with me about my faulty understanding of happiness. God rebuked me first through the lips of my son, Leon. "Mom," Leon had bluntly asked me one day, "why do you always look so unhappy?" It was true, devastatingly true, that the joy had seeped out of my life, and I complained to the Lord.

"Nothing is turning out as I had planned. Why, Lord? Why did you take away my happiness?"

God began to show me his answers to the problem of my misery. The verse he used was James 4:3: "Ye ask, and receive not, because ye ask amiss. . . ."

"But Lord," I protested, "I'm just asking you for happiness. What's wrong with that? How is that asking amiss? You want me to be happy, don't you? Your Word is full of talk about how Christians should be happy."

"Yes, my child," he seemed to answer. "I want you to be happy, overflowing with irrepressible joy, but that joy is only a by-product. It comes when you seek something else."

"What, Lord?"

"My will, Valetta, my will."

Now I came to verse 10, "Humble yourselves in the sight of the Lord, and he shall lift you up." That verse had my name on it. "Lord," I prayed, "please forgive my self-pity and self-centered life. All I think about are *my* problems. Please change me, and help me to live for you." Then I added, "Lord, I totally relinquish to you my ideas of what I think life should be, and I ask you to give me your ideas."

My prayers began to change. As I tried each day to make pleasing God the goal of my life, it occurred to me that since Jesus came to save lost, despairing people, it would please him if I would spend time reaching out to those same needy and unloved people, telling them about his life, death, and resurrection.

I realized with a jolt that doing this would indeed be "witnessing." I had heard that word thundered from my husband's pulpit. It was what every Christian should do, must do, to show that he or she was spiritual. *Witness.* That meant going out into public places, collaring people, warning them of hell and judgment, urging them to repent. *Witness.* The word evoked both guilt and fear in me. That seemed strange because telling others about Jesus was witnessing, and that was what God wanted me to do.

As soon as I felt ready to concentrate my life's focus on ministry, God brought into my life the exact person I needed to meet. Her name was Kathy Rice, now Mrs. Bruce Narramore, and she was on the staff of Campus Crusade for Christ.

Kathy, it seemed, was everything I was not. She was friendly, outgoing, and, above all, self-confident. Where she had strengths, I had nothing but weaknesses. But God had already made himself clear on that subject: the whole point of what he was doing in me was to perfect his power through my weakness.

"Kathy," I asked timidly, "would you mind going with me to the park down the street and letting me watch as you share your faith with someone?"

"Wow, I would love that, Valetta," Kathy said enthusiastically. "Now, what we wear is important," she explained. "Let's dress casually. We don't want to appear *too* different. People might think we have problems, not answers."

Astonished, I watched Kathy share her faith with a young mother. Her approach was neither preachy nor intimidatingly know-it-all. After some small talk, Kathy casually had said, "May I share something with you which has helped me a lot, and see if it makes sense to you?"

"Well, sure," came the reply, "why not?"

Can witnessing really be that simple? I asked myself.

The next Sunday I noticed an attractive Spanish-American lady who looked about my age and had slipped into the back of our Sunday school class. The Holy Spirit nudged me, and after class I greeted the woman. Nervously and with reserve, I tried to remember how Kathy would have begun. But then I began to feel a powerful love rising from deep within me and reaching out to this woman.

"Have you ever had the wonderful experience of knowing God in a personal way?" I blurted out.

She looked at me intently. "You know," she said, "I've been trying to find God in a personal way for a long, long time." Excited, I opened my Bible and began to explain God's simple plan of salvation. When I invited her to pray a sinner's prayer, she responded with joy. We became friends.

God's promise was being fulfilled in a way that exceeded all my expectations. As I tried to please him, not myself, my life brimmed with a happiness and exuberance that I had not known before.

God began regularly to point out specific individuals with whom he wanted me to share his Good News. I once made an appointment to witness to a relative and discovered another heart already prepared.

A few doors down from me lived a professional woman. The clothes she wore, the tilt of her head, suggested a worldly-wise self-assurance. She was a Hollywood photographer. I had been told she was an atheist. Inviting her over one day, we made small talk over coffee.

Summoning my courage, I said, "I've made a discovery that has helped me a lot, and since you are obviously an intelligent person, I wonder if you would listen and see if it makes sense to you."

"Of course," she responded, "please share your discovery with me."

I did, and she did not agree with all I said. She objected vigorously to some of it, but when she left, we were friends. The seed had been planted, and God would water it, I trusted.

I received an invitation to speak at a women's retreat, and other invitations followed. With the help of a journalist friend from Portland, I put together a slide presentation with taped narration and background music; it dramatized the sadness of people who live and die without the opportunity of once hearing of Christ. Incredible as it seemed, God was using me, Valetta Steel. In dying to my own pursuit of happiness, I had discovered the true source of joy.

SIX

A Widow's Seeds of Vision

In May 1972, I left Los Angeles. My car was part of a caravan, an odd assortment of vehicles moving like a giant caterpillar toward OMS Headquarters in Greenwood, Indiana, a thriving suburb of Indianapolis. In 1921, mission founders Charles and Lettie Cowman had originally located in southern California in the hope that Mr. Cowman, a dying man, would benefit from the mild climate. Since the bulk of OMS constituency had for many years been concentrated in the Midwest, the move back to Indiana was unquestionably sound strategy. It situated the mission command center close to supporting churches and key institutions.

In Greenwood, I moved into missions housing across the street from headquarters. I soon found a warm welcome in a thriving downtown church pastored by a dynamic young minister, Don Riggs. When neighborhood youth stopped by my home, I began to put into practice the principles God had given me for reaching out to confused and hurting young people. Sundays, we would load the kids into a car and take them to hear Don preach.

"Look, Valetta," Pastor Riggs said to me one day. "I've noticed that everywhere you go you've got young people with you. I think God has given you a gift of relating to youth. How about taking over our college and career Sunday school class?"

I caught my breath as I felt the old fears of inadequacy surging back over me. Satan brought to mind a vivid rerun of my earlier Sunday school teaching fiasco, reminding me that I had so firmly concluded that I was not cut out to be a teacher. As I paused, groping for words, the One who "hath not given us the spirit of fear" (2 Tim. 1:7) reminded me that taking my weaknesses and turning them into his strengths is what the Christian life is about. "Forgive me, Lord," I whispered. And then in a voice that I hoped sounded full of confidence and enthusiasm, I said, "Sure, Don, I'd be thrilled to take the class."

Sunday mornings presented me with a

challenge I had never experienced before. I recalled the scores of times I had sat in Sunday school class bored, because there was little opportunity for participation. It was my hope that every student would become a teacher, and that each would feel responsible to share spiritual insights. Since the teacher usually learns more than the students, I wanted to find ways to help each class member share in leadership. I began with polls of their current interest topics.

Could I risk a new teaching approach? Believing I should try, I chose eight people to lead discussion groups—approximately half the class—and my main responsibility was to guide the student leaders. It was then that the class doubled, and finally tripled. The Holy Spirit, I discovered, is the dynamic Teacher.

Exhausted and excited, I was discovering a spiritual principle that was new for me. Whatever investment I made in these lives was being returned manyfold. Every week I met young people with eager hearts and questioning minds—medical students, a lawyer, nurses, lab technicians, clerks, secretaries. Each life I touched left me somehow enriched, changed. God was taking a timid widow, stretching and enlarging her.

My sister Lea Ullom and her husband, Virgil, were living on the campus of Indiana

University where Virgil was studying dentistry. When I dropped in on them periodically, God opened doors for more contact with I. U. students. Their home became an informal student fellowship center.

My class at the church continued to grow as members became involved in leadership and brought their friends, many from broken homes and a few on drugs. One young man, Joey, was really spaced out. His lifeless, vacant stare bore witness to the debilitating effect of drugs. In time, I watched with a growing excitement as the Word of God penetrated the fog of Joey's mind. He became a discussion leader eventually.

My neighbor, Judy Ike, once brought a friend, George, a football player at the local high school. When George trusted Christ as Savior, he was so eager to share his newfound faith that he became one of my teaching assistants. Rick, recently returned from Vietnam, was broken, guilt-ridden, demoralized by drugs, and he soon joined our class. The class witnessed high drama as God's power rebuilt his shattered life, vividly illustrating 2 Corinthians 5:17: "Therefore, if anyone is in Christ, he is a new creation; the old has gone, the new has come!" (NIV). Leon soon discovered he had acquired a big brother in Rick—an added blessing from God.

Another young man, Steve, was a psychology major and a bit of a skeptic. Steve had gone to Sunday school as a child, but by the time he joined my class, he had concluded that the Bible was "hardly relevant" to the needs of modern man. And yet, he found himself trying to account for the profound effects the Word was having on the lives of people like Rick and Joey. He was doing some deep thinking; he dusted off his Bible and began reading it again.

One afternoon he called me on the phone. "Valetta, I see it so clearly," he began, his voice trembling with emotion. "I have been reading James, and what he said two thousand years ago about so many things seems so relevant today."

In a flash Steve had seen in James 1:22-25 that real learning takes place not merely through reason and introspection—mental processes—but by applying truth, living it out in human life. This insight became a driving force for Steve and his wife, Sharon, as they shared Christ with friends and became class discussion leaders.

Steve insisted that so many people were studying the Bible, but that they were not really learning because they hadn't learned to apply the principles. Faith grows only as it is used, he would say. As their vision broadened, Steve and Sharon began a ministry of prison evangelism. Then they started a program to teach high school students in the church to share their faith. The students included Leon and Lorna.

Meanwhile, at OMS Headquarters, I worked for the vice-president of home ministries, Merv Heebner. My job consisted of typing, filing, answering the phone, writing, and assisting in various programs—all indispensable services. I saw the importance of OMS: a Christian organization with more than three hundred missionaries on thirteen fields in Asia, Latin America, and Europe.

Certainly this was an important ministry I had been performing, I assured myself. And yet I sensed a growing restlessness, as though God were again nudging me. "What does this mean, Lord?" I asked. "Is this restlessness simply my human impatience? If you want me to continue in the office routine, I am content to do that for your glory; but Lord, if you have something more, I am willing, and I am listening."

With a vacation coming up, I had planned a two-week tour of our OMS field in Haiti, a forlorn, corruption-ridden republic six hundred miles from the coast of Florida, with the lowest per capita income of any country in the world. Accompanying me would be my sister Lea and her husband, Virgil, soon to be graduated from dental school, and a young doctor, Esther Schubert, who was completing her medical training at I. U. All three were seeking God's place for their future service. The brief trip was destined to, in different ways, dramatically alter each of our lives. In Haiti, Esther would meet her future husband, Lea and Virgil would discover God's place for them, and I would find a new calling.

The moment we disembarked from our comfortable womb of a Pan American jet, we were plunged into an environment so shockingly different, we might as well have been in the heart of Africa rather than ninety minutes from Miami. We threaded our way through the streets, crowded with small vehicles, animals, and people. We were jostled by dark bodies, and small hands were thrust at us. "Five cents, missus. This way, missus," I heard.

Aboard the mission van, we bumped along over a rutted highway that snaked through rugged mountains shrouded with mist, through dilapidated villages and collections of mud huts covered with straw or corrugated tin roofs. There were forlorn women preparing scraps of food over open fires, while naked children, bellies bloated, were playing in the dirt.

Our old rattletrap vehicle carried us past

fields of sugar cane and forests of mahogany trees, eventually taking us to the center of OMS work on the island. Here were some substantial concrete buildings, radio studios, missionary homes, a clinic, a church, and a school.

The following day, Mardy Picazo, one of the missionaries who had pioneered the Haiti work, showed us through the Emmaus Vocational Bible School. We observed bright-faced, alert young people learning basic agricultural and industrial skills along with the Scriptures. "These young people have found Christ in our churches," Mardy explained. "Most of their families live in mud houses or grass huts."

Beyond the church we came to the OMS Bethesda Clinic where we saw long lines of people patiently waiting for medical attention. One mother had brought a small baby who was nearly dead from malnutrition. As nurses fed the listless infant with a dropper, the mother hungrily licked the milk that dribbled down her baby's chin. We saw missionaries working side by side with trained Haitians, administering doses of compassion and comfort along with medicine. Periodically a pastor and a nurse joined in prayer for these Haitians or invoked the power of Jesus' name for deliverance from evil spirits.

Sunday morning we made our way down a narrow dirt path to a "brush arbor" church. We found that these simple wooden structures, covered with branches, served as temporary churches until more permanent structures could be built. As we took our seats on the narrow boards that served as benches, the Haitian pastor led the congregation in a hymn. Voiced in swelling, rhythmical Creole, the radiant, mahogany-colored countenances contrasted darkly with the sad, gaunt faces of the voodoo-haunted people we had seen in the market places.

The Haiti experience was crucial in all of our lives. By the time our two weeks were up, and we boarded the plane for the return trip to Indianapolis, Virgil and Lea had offered their lives to God in service to the Haitian people. Virgil visualized the establishment of a dental clinic—a dream that would one day be beautifully realized.

But in the meantime, before Virgil had his diploma and he and Lea had left Indiana University, was there not something God wanted them to do? I. U. was not Haiti, but it certainly was a "place to witness." All about them students faced emotional and spiritual problems, and many marriages were disintegrating. All of us felt burdened for this college community, and I began to wonder how God wanted to use us there.

I had recently read an article in *Moody Monthly* magazine that described how Christian women had been inviting neighbors over for coffee and then proceeding to share Christ with them. Sometimes an outstanding professional woman, with whom these housewives could identify, would give her witness. The neighborhood coffees had proven remarkably effective in reaching women for Jesus Christ.

Would a coffee work in an academic community? I wondered. There was only one way to find out. Virgil, Lea, and I set a date, secured a room on campus, and sent out one hundred invitations.

Only four people responded, indicating they were interested in coming, and all were Christians. Our noble project turned out to be one gigantic washout, and we canceled the event. As we sat commiserating, it dawned on me that God was bringing something good out of this. To begin with, we had acquired four new friends, and as we shared our burden with them, they all expressed a desire to be a part of our team.

Furthermore, we discovered that we had made three strategic errors. We had not checked the campus calendar and had inadvertently scheduled our coffee on the night of the big dance. Secondly, we had not delivered invitations personally and thus decided that next time, all invitations would be delivered face to face or by phone. Finally, it occurred to us that the genius of the women's coffees lay partly in the fact that they were held in homes, not in intimidating church buildings or public halls. We determined, therefore, to seek a casual atmosphere where it would be natural and easy to open up and talk about one's faith.

Immediately we set about planning another coffee. Lea and I and our new friends met to pray for the ones God would have us invite. Then we went door-to-door, until seventeen people had promised to attend. We also arranged for baby-sitting and a child evangelism program for the children since there would be twenty-three children coming too.

The evening was of tremendous encouragement to our faith. We invited Ann Wall, wife of a local dentist, to come and share her testimony. In a quiet, unassuming way, she told how Jesus Christ had revolutionized her home. Four of the group invited Christ into their lives, and the next week Lea started a Bible study in her home. "Now it seems like the whole neighborhood has changed," Lea had told me. "That coffee really broke the ice. All around women are opening their hearts to me. They are anxious to talk about spiritual things. These were the same women who hardly spoke to me when I passed them a few weeks ago."

That June, Virgil graduated from dental school. He and Lea applied to OMS and were accepted as missionaries to Haiti. As candidates they faced a staggering challenge. They would be required to raise full support: enough funds to cover all personal and ministry needs for five years plus another $6,000 for Virgil's dream of a Haitian dental clinic.

As I pondered the challenge Virgil and Lea faced, I found myself asking, "Lord, what can I do to help?"

"How about using the coffees?" the answer came back. Why not use coffees to get people involved in reaching a world for Christ? Invite neighbors to come over some evening and meet the missionary, have the candidate share his testimony, and then give people an opportunity to be involved in that ministry by sharing in his support.

It was the first step of a plan that God would use to help put scores of missionaries on the field. "Well, why not, Lord," I said. "That first coffee was a monumental flop, and yet you brought good out of it. Turning weaknesses and failures into strengths and blessings is what you specialize in."

I sat down with Lea, and together we listed the names of thirty-five people we wanted to invite. Then came the important part: getting a verbal commitment from as many of those thirty-five as possible. I picked up the phone and began calling, feeling at first uncomfortable, like a nagging telephone salesman pushing magazine subscriptions.

"Lord," I said, "keep reminding me this is for your glory and for your kingdom."

"I'm having my sister and brother-in-law over to my house," I would begin. "I'm wondering if you would like to join us and hear how Christ is working in their lives, and also about their plan to go to Haiti. Also, we can get better acquainted." Some of the contacts had conflicting engagements, but many responded positively.

"Look, Leon, I need your help," I announced to my son the afternoon before that first coffee for missions. "I am expecting maybe thirty people tonight. I want you to set up the chairs."

"Good grief, Mom, thirty!" Leon protested, falling back onto the sofa. "You'll never get thirty in here."

"Maybe not," I said, "but I want thirty chairs ready if we need them. Just stack them up."

That night twenty-five showed up. We sat them on dining room chairs, the piano bench, the folding chairs Leon had brought over from the OMS social hall; five eased themselves down on our long, low, comfortable sofa. After coffee, a snack, and an informal get-acquainted time, I asked Virgil to tell something of the direction God had given to Lea and him.

Virgil began by recalling his youthful encounter with Jesus Christ. He talked about his decision to study dentistry and then went on to describe how Haiti had broken his heart, leaving him with a burden to build a dental clinic there.

As he spoke, I scanned the faces around the room. Skepticism had melted into friendly appreciation. Other faces seemed to reflect a deep conviction. God was using a simple testimony of all-out commitment to Jesus Christ to create spiritual hunger.

As Virgil continued, I suddenly heard an ominous cracking sound. It was coming from the leg of our overburdened sofa, which wobbled pitifully for an instant, collapsed unceremoniously, and deposited its five occupants on the floor. "Lord," I shot up a prayer, "what now? This is not the way I planned it at all!"

But my confusion and embarrassment were swallowed up by the waves of laughter which engulfed our gathering. With the sofa propped up, Lea began sharing her testimony, telling how her own vision coincided with her husband's. Then the questions came from the floor: What can we do to help you get to Haiti? How about building the clinic? Do you need help with that?

That was the beginning of our mission coffees. Families and individual women began opening their homes. "Come on over," they would urge their neighbors. "We're having a friend here that we'd like you to meet. They have shared Christ overseas and would like to tell how he is relevant to their own lives and to people of other cultures."

I hardly dreamed how God would one day use this simple idea of neighborhood coffees to help scores of missionaries get to the field, and in the process restore homes and reshape many lives, mine among them.

SEVEN
A Celebrated Grief

While God continued to bless my own life through the ministry he had prepared for me, I struggled at home with my two growing children. I was encountering the often dizzying effects of trying to be a successful single parent.

The year we moved from Los Angeles to Greenwood, Leon had turned twelve, Lorna ten. The following year was Leon's thirteenth, and as though right on cue, subtle yet alarming changes began to take place. What had happened to the usually sweet-tempered, quiet little boy, who, in spite of occasional ruckuses with his sister, was usually eager to please Mom?

Suddenly in Leon's eyes, Mom had become Public Enemy Number One. When his tall, gangly frame, topped by a head of thick black hair, appeared in the doorway each afternoon after school, the atmosphere of our apartment became charged with tension. With hardly a grunt in reply to my artificially cheerful, "How was the day?" he would retreat to his room to blow his trombone in noisy protest.

When I insisted he straighten his room, which increasingly looked like a disaster area—littered with the debris of books, pieces of artwork, a dismantled radio—he shot back glares of resentment. "Why are you always on my back? You never treat Lorna this way."

Gifted musically, Leon was well on his way to mastering the trombone and guitar, but now his musical tastes veered toward harsh contemporary sounds with a frenetic beat. Entering the living room, he would turn off the easy-listening station I preferred, supplanting it with a rock station at almost full volume.

"Mom, does it have to be so loud?" Lorna would shriek. When I objected, Leon would fix me with a hurt look that seemed to accuse, "Go ahead. Order me around. Treat me like a little kid. Take away the little joy I have. Just make me more miserable."

Every mother feels pain when she realizes she must relinquish her boy in order to let him become a man. Now, when I would throw an arm around Leon in an affectionate hug, he would pull away, obviously feeling uncomfortable. And kisses from Mom were certainly taboo.

He now regarded the kitchen as a female domain, and my efforts to enlist his cooperation in the dishwashing chores began to meet with resistance. Yes, Leon was thirteen and wishing he were twenty-one. More and more Leon sought unconsciously to take his place as the man of the house. When I had women friends over for a meal or invited them to a family outing, Leon smoldered with resentment, as though another adult presence somehow threatened his place of leadership in the family structure.

"Hey, Mom!" he exploded one day after my friends had left. "If you want to have your friends over all the time, I think I might as well move out."

Increasingly Leon began to challenge my authority. Why should he always be obliged to submit to someone who had so many shortcomings herself? he reasoned. Overnight he had acquired an amazing acumen, a gift for ruthlessly discerning every inconsistency in adults, and particularly in me. He was not slow to point out these inconsistencies.

"Well, how come you are asking me to take out the garbage this week, when last week you said I didn't have to?" he would ask.

"Oh, I forgot that, Leon," I would put in lamely.

"Yeah, Mom, and that's another thing. You have a terrible memory. You are always forgetting things."

I had heard from other mothers that girls are usually easier to raise than boys. Now I discovered what they had been talking about. While from the outset Lorna had been endowed with an indomitable will, this personality trait had been balanced with level-headedness, a generous portion of good sense, and a sunny disposition that made her a friend to everyone.

Affectionate and warm as Lorna was, there was an obvious, intimate mother-daughter bond between us, which gave rise to Leon's accusation, "You always favor Lorna." Spending time with Lorna provided a panacea for all her problems. So we did things together; we cooked, sewed, raised dogs, and worked on child-evangelism projects.

While Leon was moody, Lorna was outgoing, action-oriented, full of initiative and self-confidence. From her father, I thought, she had inherited strong leadership qualities, combined with a fertile imagination. Her creative mind teemed with ideas—a cookout, an impromptu drama, a pajama party.

Responsible beyond her years, she had proved herself a trusted baby-sitter, and on one occasion she cared for a neighbor's children for a month while the woman completed her master's thesis. At school, she exceeded any parent's expectations, and had even skipped a grade when we had moved to California. She habitually respected authority figures, parents, teachers, and yet had the strength of character to disagree with a teacher who used vulgar language in class.

In short, Lorna was a model daughter—the kind of sister my struggling Leon could not help but resent. The summer following his freshman year Leon announced, "You know, Mom, I think I'd like to leave home"; and then he added wistfully, "I really would leave home if I could support myself." He said finally, "But since I can't yet, I guess I'll just have to stick around."

Repeatedly, as I imagine many a baffled Christian parent has done, I would retreat to my bedroom and fall on my knees, pouring out my heart to God. "Lord, how I need Henry now, and Leon needs him—where are you in all this, Lord? I am so weak. Right here, Lord, in this business of parenting, I need you to take my weakness and turn it into your strength. I need answers. I don't know what to do. I have never raised adolescents before. What am I doing wrong? Where do I need to change? You said in your Word, 'If any of you lack wisdom, let him ask.' Well, I lack wisdom, Lord. And I am asking."

Gradually insights came, and I began to make some changes. I realized I had always seen myself as a "helping person." In my unique roles as mother and leader of the home, I had always tried to be a peacemaker, but had been reluctant to show a firm hand in exerting leadership and giving clear direction. I learned that kids need limits and confident direction.

Now, when it came to matters I felt were essential to their personal growth, instead of asking, "Do you want to do this or that?" I said, "I *expect* you to do this." There wouldn't be many rules, but I would be consistent in enforcing the few I made. These rules would be laid down without apologies: loud music for only one hour, no TV during dinners so we can hold intelligent conversations. Surprisingly, Leon and Lorna accepted my new stance—in fact, they seemed to welcome it.

Keeping the lines of communication open, a basic principle in all human relationships, is not easily achieved when dealing with adolescents who suddenly have a penchant for privacy. Still, I would work on it. "How did school go today?" often inspired monosyllabic responses; but there were, I discovered, topics that would provoke at least a modicum of intelligent oral response—sports, music, certain school activities, and their friends. Leon was actually interested in politics, I even discovered.

Next came the hard part. "Confess your faults to one another," the Bible says (James 5:16). But did that mean that I should confess them to my children? I decided it did. They had already detected plenty of human frailties in me and had seen through my phoniness; why not talk about those frailties and solicit their help?

With God's help I did. I admitted my faults, yes, my sins, to my own children; I confessed those sins and asked for Leon's and Lorna's forgiveness. I soon discovered that hearing Mom confess her faults gave them the freedom to acknowledge problem areas in their own lives.

Finally, God showed me I needed to place Leon's future entirely in the Lord's hands. Was I hanging onto a dream that Leon would someday be a minister like Henry, or at least a full-time Christian worker? In my circle of friends, having a child in the ministry or on the mission field seemed to be the ultimate parental accomplishment. Could I accept Leon as a salesman, an artist, a secular musician? "Lord, I surrender," I prayed. "He is yours. Do with him whatever you want. I just ask that he love you, live for you in whatever career you have chosen for him."

God was teaching me through my frustrations with Leon. He seemed to be saying, "Can you praise me for what I am doing in Leon? Praise—by faith—even when you see little to be encouraged about?" As I cultivated a thankful, praiseful heart, I began to notice positive qualities in Leon, and I learned to give sincere compliments without embarrassing my son or myself.

"Would you like to know what Leon shared in our youth meeting last night?" one of the young people from church asked me one day.

"Of course," I replied.

"Well," he continued, "Leon said, 'I miss my dad a lot, but I am finding that Jesus can be closer than a dad, and he's my best friend.'"

Leon began to use his musical gifts to express his love for Christ. He, Lorna, and a neighbor, Cindy Burr, started singing together. They joined The SPARCS, a church musical group, often in demand for Christian concerts. Their exuberant music, in praise to Jesus Christ, regularly brought troubled young people to the Savior.

Friends commented on leadership qualities they saw in Leon. He was elected president of the church youth group, and he enthusiastically performed on a winning Bible quiz team. An aptitude test indicated that he had outstanding abilities in verbal skills and music. "Mom," he announced one day, after a stirring address by Korean missionary Dr. Ed Kilbourne, "I think the Lord may be calling me to Korea as a youth worker."

"Lord," I whispered, "I see you are still in the miracle business."

Praising God for such miracles came so easily. Yet the miracles also provided a painful contrast to the sudden deaths of Leon and Lorna. Thus, when the uniformed officer appeared at my door that cold February evening, the full impact of his words gradually penetrated my brain with a violent, paralyzing force. "Your children and their friend have just been killed." It was as though I were standing outside myself, a spectator to some gruesome drama. Certainly, in a moment, I would awaken from the nightmare.

With Danny and Henry, the valley had approached more gradually. I had had time to prepare, to brace myself for the dark, irrevocable finality of the loss; but this time the valley had come upon me suddenly, sucking me down, down into the blackness in one vicious gulp. And yet, even as my brain reeled under the impact, deep from within my being welled up the sweet, mysterious consciousness of the Presence, the everlasting arms: "Yea, though I walk through the valley of the shadow of death, I will fear no evil" (Ps. 23:4).

Thus, the words came almost unbidden to my lips, "Officer, I know where they are. They are with God." As I closed the door behind me a surge of comfort came from the realization too that God had prepared a spiritual family to stand with me in my hour of trial. *Who should I call first? Flo Rickards.* Flo had stayed with Lorna on our world trip. Through the years she had been a friend who had worked with the church youth, and had been close to the children. I picked up the phone. "Flo," I began shakily, "the children have just been killed in an accident. I need you. Can you come?"

Flo came, as did my precious neighbors, Les and Pat Ike, my boss, Merv Heebner, and his wife, Clara. They embraced me, and we wept together and prayed. Only those who are part of the body of Christ can know and understand the sweetness of this kind of consolation in the dark moments of life.

When news reached my sister Lea in Haiti, they were entertaining a team of laymen visiting the field on an evangelistic crusade. Immediately the crusaders took up an offering to fly Lea home. Ordinarily flights were fully booked and reservations had to be made well in advance, but on this day it "just happened" that one seat was available.

When Lea came in the front door, and we embraced, she could sense that God was already doing something special. "Valetta," she said, "why you, of all people? I don't understand it, but I know God is doing something eternal for his glory, and I can already sense he has done something special in you."

I sensed at this time I was being supernaturally sustained by the Spirit of God and by the supporting, consoling love of my spiritual brothers and sisters. Still, a dark shadow would now and then flit across my mind. *Soon*, I thought, *I will come crashing down, crushed and wounded and helpless*. I felt I would be haunted, as though an old wound had been freshly opened; I would again experience the void left by the loss of my firstborn and the depression that came in the wake of Henry's death. Then God spoke a word of gentle rebuke. "If I can sustain you today," he said, "can't you trust me with tomorrow?"

As news of the children's deaths was broadcast on TV and radio and conveyed by phone to friends all over the world, I sensed that I was being borne aloft on a surging tide of prayer and love. I have never known love like that. The world seemed literally to be dripping love, oozing at every pore. Was this the mysterious essence of Calvary— that love in all its sublime glory can in mortal minds only be understood when there is a cross? I wondered if others could discern the divine paradox the Spirit of God was enacting in the mortal life of Valetta Steel: that God never loves his children so dearly as when he lets them suffer. He never walks with them as closely as when he escorts them through the valley.

As I knew myself the special object of the love and prayers of God's people, I felt humbled as never before. What had I done to deserve this? Nothing, absolutely nothing. It was all of him, and suddenly I grasped the meaning of grace in a new way.

The morning following the children's death, it was as though God had pulled back a curtain and let me peek into heaven. It was all joy. Leon and Lorna were there and saying, "Mother, won't you share our joy? Dad is here and our brother, too. We're celebrating. Won't you celebrate with us?"

As I envisioned the funeral, I began to feel a growing conviction that it should be a glad celebration. Leon and Lorna knew Jesus and loved him. They had lived for him unashamedly and had shared his good news with others. Their Lord had summoned them (who are we to say prematurely?) to their blessed and eternal home. Was that not cause for celebration?

But I hesitated. Some would not understand. What would they think of a mother who wanted to celebrate her children's deaths? Crazy? Unnatural? Morbid? Irreverent? Could they see what I saw? Later that morning a group of young people from the church came by. I shared with them the idea of turning the funeral into a celebration. "You know," they responded, "that is exactly what we have been feeling. We hesitated to suggest it, not knowing how you would react."

So we planned a celebration. The SPARCS would sing some of the joyful, exultant songs Leon and Lorna had loved, and I invited our MFM (Men for Missions) friend, Tom Gold, to sing "The King Is Coming."

Flo Rickards accompanied me to the funeral home. When the caskets were opened, I felt puzzled. What had they done to Leon? Had his face been so mutilated that they had had to rebuild it? Whoever it was in that casket, it did not look like my son. "Is his hair combed right? Does he look natural?" the mortician was asking.

"Something is not right," I muttered. "This is not Leon, is it?"

Flo put in, "There is some mistake." Indeed, there had been a mistake. In the aftermath of the accident, Leon's body had been switched with that of his friend, Don Prock, and sent to Don's home in Iowa.

So now arrangements had to be made hastily to rectify the mistake. This could have been very upsetting had my heart not been soothed by the comforting knowledge that Leon had already discarded his earthly shell and was now enjoying the freedom and perfection of his resurrected body.

Leon and Lorna's celebration was the triumphant, joyful, and unmistakable witness to their faith and was all that we had envisioned it would be. Afterwards, several church young people approached me. "I hope you won't misunderstand what I am saying," one began, "but it is a good thing it was them and not me because they were ready and I wasn't. I was faking it, but I want you to know that today I completely surrendered my life to Jesus Christ." Others told how as a result of the children's deaths they had recommitted their lives to Jesus.

Dr. Long, a professor at Greenville College, wrote, "Although we cannot see it with our finite minds, we know God never makes mistakes, and only eternity will reveal the total results of this seeming tragedy. It has affected every student in the school, we believe."

The morning after the funeral my phone rang, and I heard the voice of a troubled young woman on the line. "I saw a newspaper on the floor and was startled," she said. "Could it really be your children?"

"Yes," I replied, "they were my children. It is a terrible loss, but I am celebrating because they are with Jesus and were ready to meet him."

Then I heard sobbing. "You know, Mrs. Steel, I'm not ready to meet Christ," she said. I invited her over to my house, and that afternoon she prayed and asked Christ into her life.

As everyone who has studied the subject of grief knows, the most difficult time comes after the initial impact of the tragedy and funeral subsides, and the bereaved is no longer the object of special solicitous attention. The shock wears off, and life must go on; but how to go on in a world irrevocably changed and made stark and strange by the new uncomfortable, gaping holes created by the absence of beloved personalities?

But God had given me a promise in that hour when I had felt the love of his people pouring down upon me. "If I can take care of you today," he had whispered, "can't you trust me with tomorrow?" Well, now "tomorrow" was here.

The Spirit once more directed me to the Book of Job, and again, for the third time in my life, those precious Spirit-ordained passages performed their divine function. "Why are you using your ignorance to deny my providence?" God had said. "Where were you when I laid the foundations of the earth? Tell me, if you know so much" (Job 38:2, 4, TLB). No, there is no way that men can fully understand or fathom the providence of God. That is why he has given us the gift of faith, to believe and to leave those mysteries in his hands, until the final unveiling.

I turned to James 5:11: "We know how happy they are now because they stayed true to him then, even though they suffered greatly for it. Job is an example of a man who continued to trust the Lord in sorrow; from his experiences we can see how the Lord's plan finally ended in good, for he is full of tenderness and mercy" (TLB).

"What I did for Job," God seemed to be

saying, "I am going to do for you."

The sudden death of a loved one, particularly by accident, leaves surviving relatives with a vague, sometimes remorseless sense of guilt. Had I somehow been remiss in my parenting? Too trusting? Too permissive?

Whatever the circumstances in the accident, I found comfort in the fact that I had raised my son to be a responsible young man. He had proven himself to be a careful driver, demonstrating good judgment and integrity ever since he had gotten his license as a high school junior.

Other thoughts intruded as I did a mental playback of the children's lives and mine. Had I been a wise Christian parent, helping my kids establish their priorities, helping them sort through the confusing choices of life, distinguishing the petty from the eternal? God comforted me with the thought that the most important things had been done; Leon and Lorna had been pointed to the Savior, and they had shared their faith.

The absolute finality of death has a marvelous power to, in one swift stroke, adjust one's scale of values, which is often lost or confused in the helter-skelter process of modern life. How I thank God now that amid the relentless demands of my life, yes, even the ceaseless demands of Christian service, I had learned the importance of leading my children to a personal faith in Jesus Christ. I remember the day Lorna had asked, "Mommy, how can I know I am a Christian, and that I will go to heaven when I die?" I was profoundly grateful, now, that I had not put her off with a vague answer, but had been willing, able, and eager to lead a little child, my child, into God's kingdom.

I had honestly strived to make Christ the centerpiece of our home, and though I had failed many times, I was grateful now that I knew God honored the weak. He had enabled me to confess my faults to my children and ask their forgiveness.

What inexpressible comfort were those indelible memories of Leon and Lorna, alone in their rooms, pouring over their well-marked Living New Testaments. Though they had both been top students, what gave me joy now was the knowledge that they had counted the business of sharing Jesus with a classmate more important than getting an *A* in chemistry or English. Now there were no regrets that I had consistently taken time for friendship with my children: for cookouts, raising dogs, sewing, long conversations, even debates about sports, music, politics, and religion.

If there is one message I would like to shout to every parent, it is this: Every day that you live out your life before your children, you are imparting to them an entire value system, and what a phony set of values many parents dump on their children. Even Christian parents model life-styles characterized by money and material possessions. Such are vain and transient baubles when set in an eternal perspective. The fulfillment of selfish ambition, and the brief, fickle applause of man: how futile they will appear someday when seen in the light of eternity.

Death underscores the truth of that time-worn couplet, "Only one life, 'twill soon be past, Only what's done for Christ will last."

If you think you can convey that truth to your child on the strength of a sermonette, or on an easy, pious exhortation, you are mistaken. There is only one way that they will understand it, believe it, accept it, and begin to live it; and that is when they see you consistently modeling a Christian life-style. Whatever else life may consist of, living unashamedly for Jesus Christ and making the sharing of his Good News with a lost world, the first item on our agendas is when sound priorities are modeled.

EIGHT
Reasons of the Heart

As I share my testimony in churches, homes, and at women's retreats, the question I am most often asked is: "After all you've been through—losing a child to leukemia, a husband to Hodgkin's disease, the sudden death of your two remaining children in an automobile accident—after all that, how can you retain your faith in a loving God? How can you go on smiling, praising the Lord, talking about his goodness? It doesn't make sense."

I answer that nowhere in Scripture are we told that because we are God's children we will be spared the harsh realities of human life. The Bible says, "Yet man is born unto trouble, as the sparks fly upward" (Job 5:7). Though God showers blessings and goodness upon us without measure, it is also true that his very Son, the one he loves most, is the one he allowed to suffer the most.

God wants us to share in the character of his Son. So, even though suffering offends our shallow, human view of a loving God, the Christian who has passed through the fire learns with Pascal a high logic: "The heart has its reasons which reason cannot understand." In the business of spiritual heart surgery, God's keenest instrument is suffering. Why? Because only in dying do we learn to live and only in relinquishing everything do we know what true gain is.

Since God loves us and only allows good, we can only understand suffering in the light of the Resurrection. Resurrection power means that something positive will arise from all suffering for the Christian, just as Christ arose from the dead.

Another by-product of pain is the increasingly sweet discovery of the Holy Spirit as a Comforter in the life of God's child. Many Christians are timid and ineffective because they have not grasped this truth.

I like to think of it this way: We all have had times when we have felt low in spirit, despondent, discouraged. Then have entered a room and found a group of friends who know us, understand us, and love us. As we've sat there in that company, we've felt warmed by their friendship and love, reaching out to us with invisible arms to embrace, soothe, and uplift. That is parallel to the ministry of the Holy Spirit in our lives. If we recognize him and meditate on God's words of wisdom, allowing him to perform his divine work, he will be there always, teaching, encouraging, comforting, uplifting.

Why does he do this? We read in 2 Corinthians 1:4 that he is the one "who comforteth us in all our tribulation, that we may be able to comfort them which are in any trouble. . . ." We also read, "You can be sure that the more we undergo sufferings for Christ, the more he will shower us with his comfort and encouragement" (2 Cor. 1:5, TLB).

Without the presence of Christ and his Word, I would at one time have viewed suffering as punishment. I would have responded with anger, resentment, bitterness, self-pity, and depression. However, since the Word has taught me that suffering is positive, I have looked for those positive results so I can follow God's directions in 1 Thessalonians 5:16-18, TLB: "Always be joyful. Always keep on praying. No matter what happens, always be thankful, for this is God's will for you who belong to Christ Jesus."

When others ask me how to handle the long dark tunnel of despair caused by separation and suffering, I try to encourage them to develop three simple attitudes: First, develop a grateful heart by focusing on all God is going to do for you through suffering:

James 1:2-4: Our character is developing. Phil. 3:10: We will know Christ better. Heb. 10:32-34: We still have better things ahead. 2 Cor. 4:17: Our troubles are small and short compared to our eternal blessings and glory.

Second, do as Robert Schuller so aptly instructs: "Turn your scars into stars." In every problem there is a new opportunity for creative ways to reach out to others for Christ. However, to find that opportunity, we must let go of the past.

Third, discover eternal priorities and become committed to sharing Christ at home and through world missions. Millions of people are waiting for their first chance to hear of Christ.

After the home-going of Leon and Lorna, I found I had more time to give to the coffee ministry I had stumbled upon with Virgil and Lea. I wanted to reach out to neighbors, and I was increasingly convinced of the effectiveness of the ministry in involving the lay Christians in the enterprise of missions.

God was using these home coffees not only to break apathetic hearts for a lost world, but also to bring unsaved neighbors to himself. I longed to give myself more fully to this work, and I shared the burden with my supervisor, Merv Heebner.

One day Merv called me into his office. "Valetta," he said, "we feel God is doing something significant through your home meetings and that he would have us release you to give more of your time to the ministry if that is what you feel he is leading you to do. How would you like to write your own job description?"

A short time later, OMS established a home-meeting department. With the help of a friend, OMS Regional Director Wes Haines, I put together a book entitled *Home Meetings—Your Link to Your World.* The book sets out practical guidelines for successful home meetings, along with appropriate Bible study materials. We saw over a thousand families register to become involved in home coffees for missionaries.

The next ten years took me to hundreds of homes and churches in many states. I marveled as God used the simple home-meeting concept to involve thousands of lay Christians in outreach by mobilizing others through their own missionary witness in prayer, giving, and going to the field.

During these years, deep in my heart an idea had been growing that fills my life with energy and excitement. It took shape in Youngstown, Ohio, when Gary Persing, a student at Ohio State University, asked me, "If you were the only Christian in the world, would the world have a chance to hear?"

The answer to that question focuses on the importance of one individual, any individual. If you and I could disciple one Christian every year to become a missionary, and that Christian would disciple one person a year to become a multiplying disciple-maker among peoples where there is no witness, in thirty-three years one person could reach more than four billion people with the gospel. Unfortunately, at the present time it takes 2,500 Christians in America to produce one missionary. As we follow God's command to disciple others, teaching the Great Commission, not everyone responds, so it seems we all need to disciple many to see more workers out in the dark areas of the world.

Because of this vision for more workers, I believe recruitment of young people for missions is a high priority, and I sought opportunities in this area. To know there are young people who have never heard of Christ seems the greatest tragedy in all the world, and somehow it makes my problems seem very small.

As opportunities came for me to speak on Christian college campuses in behalf of overseas careers, I wanted to increase our follow-up of those who were interested. Then, in 1983 an opportunity came for me to experience a short-term mission in English evangelism in Taiwan, primarily to make my recruitment ministry more credible. However, in Taiwan, my heart became filled with love for the Chinese people and the Lord showed me a ready opportunity for discipling among new converts at the OMS center in Taichung. Here is the opportunity to prepare workers among a portion of the largest segment of the world's population, the Chinese.

"The Lord is my shepherd" (Ps. 23:1) wrote the Psalmist, and then he went on: "Yea, though I walk through the valley of the shadow of death, I will fear no evil: for thou art with me" (v. 4). My life is a resounding *Amen* to those verses. And my heart echoes an exuberant *Hallelujah* to the final testimony of another beloved verse: "Surely goodness and mercy shall follow me all the days of my life: and I will dwell in the house of the Lord forever" (Ps. 23:6).

Of course, I am celebrating because soon

I'll see Christ, my loved ones, and friends from Taiwan, India, Haiti, the U.S., and other nations of the world.

In the meantime, I will remember Paul's words: "But life is worth nothing unless I use it for doing the work assigned me by the Lord Jesus—the work of telling others the Good News about God's mighty kindness and love" (Acts 20:24, TLB.)

Other Living Books Best-sellers

WHAT WIVES WISH THEIR HUSBANDS KNEW ABOUT WOMEN by James Dobson. The best-selling author of *DARE TO DISCIPLINE* and *THE STRONG-WILLED CHILD* brings us this vital book that speaks to the unique emotional needs and aspirations of today's woman. An immensely practical, interesting guide. 07-7896 $2.95.

HINDS' FEET ON HIGH PLACES by Hannah Hurnard. A classic allegory of a journey toward faith that has sold more than a million copies! 07-1429 $3.50.

MORE THAN A CARPENTER by Josh McDowell. A hard-hitting book for people who are skeptical about Jesus' deity, his resurrection, and his claims on their lives. 07-4552 $2.95.

LOOKING FOR LOVE IN ALL THE WRONG PLACES by Joe White. Using wisdom gained from many talks with young people, White steers teens in the right direction to find love and fulfillment in a personal relationship with God. 07-3825 $2.95.

ROCK by Bob Larson. A well-researched and penetrating look at today's rock music and rock performers, their lyrics, and their life-styles. 07-5686 $2.95.

GIVERS, TAKERS, AND OTHER KINDS OF LOVERS by Josh McDowell and Paul Lewis. This book bypasses vague generalities about love and sex and gets right to the basic questions: Whatever happened to sexual freedom? What's true love like? Do men respond differently than women? If you're looking for straight answers about God's plan for love and sexuality, this book was written for you. 07-1031 $2.50.

THE POSITIVE POWER OF JESUS CHRIST by Norman Vincent Peale. All his life the author has been leading men and women to Jesus Christ. In this book he tells of his boyhood encounters with Jesus and of his spiritual growth as he attended seminary and began his world-renowned ministry. 07-4914 $3.95.

MOUNTAINS OF SPICES by Hannah Hurnard. Here is an allegory comparing the nine spices mentioned in the Song of Solomon to the nine fruits of the Spirit. A story of the glory of surrender by the author of *HINDS' FEET ON HIGH PLACES*. 07-4611 $3.50.

NOW IS YOUR TIME TO WIN by Dave Dean. In this true-life story, Dean shares how he locked into seven principles that enabled him to bounce back from failure to success. Read about successful men and women—from sports and entertainment celebrities to the ordinary people next door—and discover how you too can bounce back from failure to success! 07-4727 $2.95.

HOW TO BE HAPPY THOUGH MARRIED by Tim LaHaye. One of America's most successful marriage counselors gives practical, proven advice for marital happiness. 07-1499 $2.95.

The books listed are available at your bookstore. If unavailable, send check with order to cover retail price plus $1.00 per book for postage and handling to:

Christian Book Service
Box 80
Wheaton, Illinois 60189

Prices and availability subject to change without notice. Allow 4–6 weeks for delivery.